Handwriting Analysis Self-Taught

by Joel Engel

ELSEVIER/NELSON BOOKS
New York

This book is dedicated to my mother,
Beatty Engel, without whose strength
and support this book could never
have been written. May she rest in peace.

Library of Congress Catalogue Card Number: 80-53238

Published in the United States by Elsevier/Nelson Books, a division of Elsevier-Dutton Publishing Company, Inc., New York. Published simultaneously in Don Mills, Ontario, by Nelson/Canada.

Printed in the U.S.A.   First Edition

10 9 8 7 6 5 4 3 2 1

Contents

Author's Preface

As a member of the faculty of the Diaspora Yeshiva, I was confronted by a complex problem. The success of many of our students, both academically and in matters of personality, depended upon their correct placement in our programs. How could I quickly ascertain the achievement potential of a student?

This led me to study the many methods of psychological and intellectual testing, and as I did so, I was constantly impressed by the high correlation of handwriting and personality. When I tested these graphological concepts on my students, it became apparent that I had not only arrived at a solution to student placement, but had also acquired a most valuable tool for monitoring and assisting their continuing growth and development.

As my knowledge and skill deepened, I began to see that many of the graphological concepts were consistent with my Talmudic studies. The Zohar, the fundamental text on Jewish mysticism, for instance, speaks of the "right" as male and the "left" as female. The Talmud tells us a teacher should bring his student close with his right hand and push him away with his left.

Moreover, many biblical verses refer to "up" or "the heights" as the place of spiritual aspiration, whereas "down" refers to the nether world of purgatory. In his graphological chart, Max Pulver demonstrates these concepts: right represents father, the male aspect; left, the mother, the female aspect. The upper zone represents the spiritual, and the lower zone, the physical, sensual realm.

As a result of my study and research, and after many requests from my professional colleagues, I have undertaken to write this work to aid those interested in grasping the exciting science of graphology. I have brought examples from famous people of varied cultures and endeavors to illustrate the concepts spoken of in the text.

Finally, I would like to express my deepest gratitude to the dean of the Diaspora Yeshiva, Rabbi Dr. Mordecai Goldstein, for his constant inspiration and warmth, which have been an unending source of motivation throughout our relationship.

About This Book . . .

There have been a number of books on graphology. But most of them are either too technical and thus difficult for the layman to understand, or too simplistic, so that they offer very little for the serious student of graphology. I wanted to bridge the gap.

Therefore I decided to concentrate on the formation of letters—showing them in visual aids. This will help the student grasp the subject quickly and help him to retain better what he has learned. In this way, with the tools given him, the student should be able in a short time to interpret any letters independently.

And since one of the major tasks of a person's life is to figure out just who he or she is, I hope this book will also help its readers to become more knowledgeable about themselves.

1

What Is Graphology?

Graphology is the study of handwriting and what it can tell about the mind behind it.

When a person writes, it's his hand that does the writing, but his brain that does the dictating. There have been many cases of amputees who, having lost the hand or arm with which they wrote, relearned the art with either the other hand, or the feet, or the mouth. Aside from a certain understandable shakiness caused by the difficulties of the feat, the writings were extremely similar to the originals. Trained graphologists had no trouble recognizing the same individual.

From this, we see that it is the personality that is expressed on paper by the handwriting. When a person writes in a given fashion, it represents a particular personality trait, which comes directly from the brain. Thus graphology shows the most in-depth parts of the personality.

For example, it does not reveal the age or sex of the writer, but it does show his (or her) maturity and whether his (or her) personality traits are predominantly masculine or feminine. Mature writing may be produced by a fifty-year-old man or a ten-year-old child, because it is the level of maturity that makes itself known, not the chronological age. Similarly, some graphological signs point to a "masculine" type of personality, but many women write that way—and vice versa. Some graphologists do attempt to reveal these two factors of age or

1

sex, but they are correct only 60 percent of the time, as compared to being 90–95 percent correct when dealing with psychological analysis.

Years ago, graphologists used to look for a common denominator in the handwriting of groups of people known to display a certain character trait. Having found it, they would conclude that everyone whose handwriting shows this particular idiosyncracy must possess the same personality trait. If, among five hundred people, the majority wrote a *t* bar flung to the right and had violent personalities, then it was assumed that every writer of a *t* bar flung rightward had a violent personality.

This was known as the empirical method. Although modern-day graphologists do not totally disagree with this method, they do believe that empirical facts must be handled with care. The fact that the majority of the people in a particular group write a certain way is not proof that all do. It is only an indication, a hint of what else to look for. A single handwriting trait must be only one part of a total analysis and is useful only as a brushstroke in creating the total picture.

The following is a general list of what the graphologist will look for when doing an analysis.

1. Direction (slant) of writing
2. Zones
3. *t* bars
4. *i* dots
5. Sexuality
6. Base line
7. Margins
8. Beginning and end strokes
9. Connected and disconnected writing
10. Forms of connection
11. Pressure
12. Loops
13. Letters
14. Personality traits
15. Signature
16. Physical health

The graphologist takes all the above evidence and puts it together, producing the final analysis. This will be discussed in the following chapters in more detail.

Note, please, that this book is geared in particular to the American subject. It applies to other nationalities only insofar as their national forms of handwriting are also taken into consideration. American students are taught to write with a slight inclination to the right, and I have allowed for this throughout the book. If the person whose writing you want to analyze is from some other country, you must know the slant of writing natural in his homeland and adjust the standard that will be used there to that angle. If, for example, he went to school in England, where students are taught to write at an upright angle, you must give somewhat more emphasis if his writing slants to the right than I have given here and somewhat less if his writing slants to the left.

2

The Slant

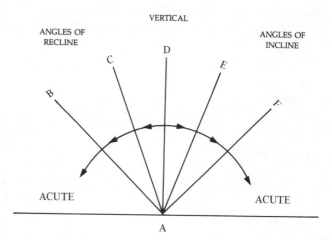

FIGURE 1.

Picture a man standing bolt upright—the very image of independence, separateness. In Figure 1, look at line AD—it is straight. When one writes in such a fashion more or less consistently, we say that his writing is vertical. In line AE, however, we have a picture of a man reaching out to speak with someone, as though he were trying to meet the other person part way.

In line AF, we see the same as line AE, only more so. Now there is almost desperation in his urge to communicate with the other party, his need for other people. AF is quite a dependent person, all but leaning on the other man for support.

In line AC, on the other hand, we see someone withdrawing from communication, cooling off, a certain amount of rebellion present.

And in line AB, we see a kind of super AC, strongly defiant, a person who wants and demands to be alone. AC leans so far away from the other person that he is nearly falling on his back.

The slant of writing is one of the most basic and important points in graphology. When you write, your intention is simple—to tell the other person what is on your mind, to communicate. When your approach is "cool," your head (as opposed to your heart) is in control. The vertical writer may indeed have intense emotions, but they are held in check.

When writing leans to the right, we call it *inclined writing*. The inclined writer moves toward the party he is dealing with. The wider the degree of inclination, the stronger the urge to communicate and the stronger the feelings in general. When the writing angle is so forward that it moves into the area marked "acute," we see a person whose emotions are almost out of control, the sensitive one who blows up at the least little thing. His line of reasoning is quite off at times, for he is too emotional to evaluate situations properly. Often he becomes jealous, sentimental, and moody, and may be in desperate need of help. His warmth makes him a likable person, but his temper can easily rage. He is also a very romantic individual.

Writing with a leftward angle of inclination is called *reclined writing* (or sometimes *backhand*). Left-hand writing (by which graphologists do not mean something written with the left hand but an angle of writing that pulls toward the left) is caused by a situation in the writer's childhood—usually a relationship with his mother and, more often than not, a negative relationship. The left-hand side in writing represents the past, and the fact that a man still writes with a leftward reclination shows that, in one way or another, he has not grown. It may be something slight (and a slight reclination), or it may have been a very powerful experience. But whatever it was, it stunted his growth to some degree, and he now withdraws, is cool.

When the writer leans into the leftward area of "acute," he is detached from society, or on his way there. This angle of writing demonstrates coldness toward others, but the coldness is actually what the writer feels within himself. He is really reverting to the womb for protection, for reassurance, for warmth. He is introverted, drawn back into himself, and thus is in retreat from the rest of the world.

It is extremely difficult to get through to the acutely left-handed writer, for he does not readily open up. He is usually quite emotional, but his emotions rarely show. To some extent this is true of all left-handed writers. AC, in general, has the emotions of AE, and AB the emotions of AF (or of someone midway between AE and AF), but unlike the inclined writers, who let their emotions out, reclined writers hold them back.

It is interesting to note that people who write with their left hand rarely write reclined, but there is a certain tendency among them to write a more vertical hand than their right-handed counterparts. Notice the handwriting samples of the ambidextrous M. K. Gandhi:

FIGURE 2A. *M K Gandhi*

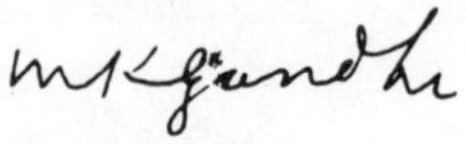

FIGURE 2B. *M K Gandhi*

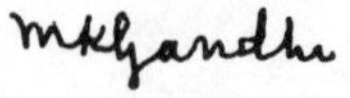

Figure 2A is written with his right hand; Figure 2B, with his left. The writing with his right hand slants to the right, whereas the writing with the left is vertical.

Although a graphologist cannot with absolute certainty determine whether a particular writer is left-handed or right-handed (in the normal sense), there are hints. For instance, in the majority of cases, when a right-handed writer crosses the *t* bar, the left side of the bar will be thicker and the right side thinner (Figure 3). The writer's mind is on the next word, so he quickly eases up on the pressure and races on, and this is true of the left-handed writer as well. But the latter usually crosses the *t* bar from right to left, so the right side of the *t* bar will be thicker and the left side thinner (Figure 4).

FIGURE 3.   FIGURE 4.

What we have said about the fiery emotions of the acutely inclined writer holds true also for AF, but not so severely. Conversely, the cold withdrawal of the acutely reclined writer is similar to AB's state of mind, but to a lesser degree.

Even the AD writer is not without problems. His control over his emotions may be so complete that it is not easy for him to show feelings when they are needed. The healthiest writing is somewhere between AD and AE. The head is in control, and yet the writer is not completely detached emotionally.

In the United States the writing that is taught in school is called the Palmer Method. This is a round writing leaning to the right. When we examine handwriting, we look to see how much and in what ways the writer has deviated from this method. Variations give the graphologist much information as to the nature of the writer. No American school teaches left-hand writing, so when we see backhand, we understand how strong the person's rebellion must be.

The so-called "coolness" of the Englishman seems to be expressed in his vertical handwriting. In Germany, until recently, students were taught an inclined writing in an angular hand (round writing is "soft" writing, angular writing is "hard, rigid"), and many people felt this represented the "blood and iron" of the German national character.

One last note about reclined writers. Because their personalities are usually negative, among the male reclined writers we find a certain degree of femininity; likewise, in the women, a certain degree of masculinity. The leftward inclination represents something opposite to one's true identity.

In spite of the inclined angle his generation was taught, note that the famed revolutionary Karl Marx, author of *The Communist Manifesto*, wrote with a leftward slant:

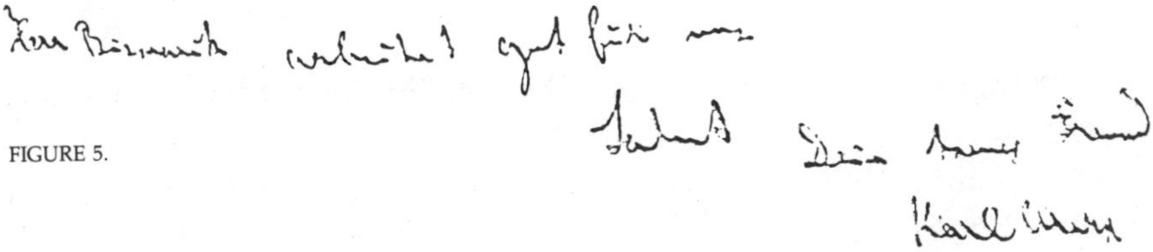

FIGURE 5.

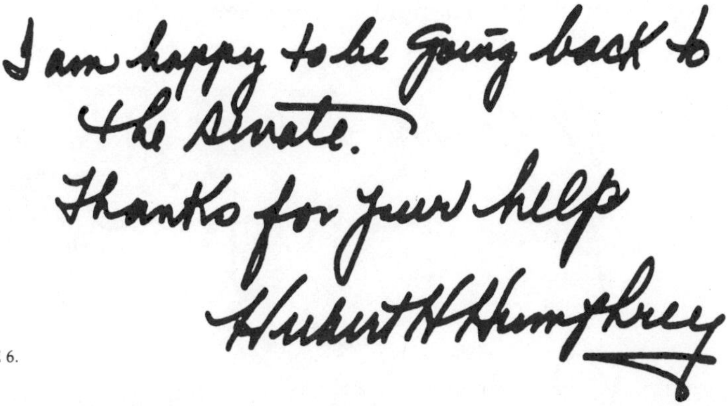

FIGURE 6.

In Figure 6, we have the right-slanted writing, with heavy pressure (to be discussed in a later chapter) of the late Sen. Hubert H. Humphrey. From his script we see his gesture of reaching out toward others, a most warm personality. We also notice quite similar traits in the handwriting of Simon Bolivar (Figure 7):

FIGURE 7.

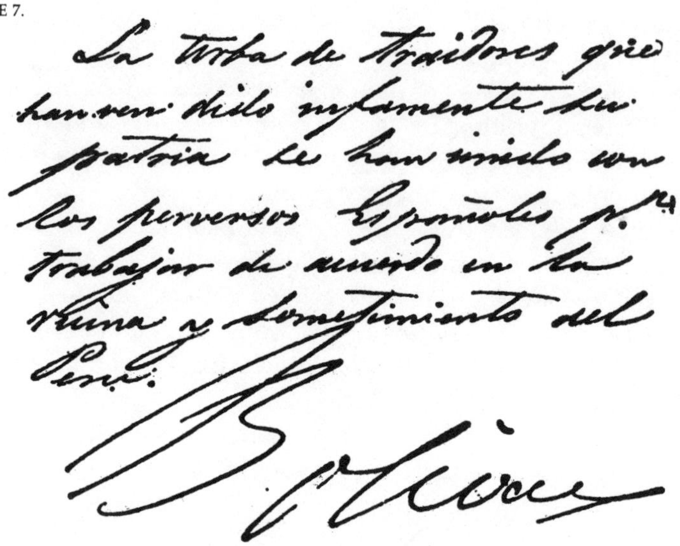

Though the body of the writing (Figure 8A) slants a bit to the right, we see by the signature of Ronald Reagan (Figure 8B), which is vertical, a certain degree of "coolness." In all fairness it must be said that this signature was written quite a few years after the writing took place, so it may be said that he has gone from a "reaching out toward the people" campaign to a more conservative position.

FIGURE 8A.

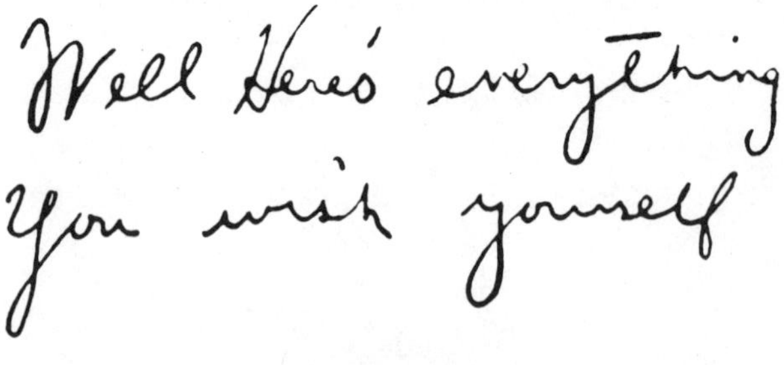

FIGURE 8B.

3

The Zones

The authoritative Swiss graphologist Max Pulver (1889–1952) composed the chart below, showing many of the points discussed in the previous chapter. But in addition to demonstrating slant, it also demonstrates the zones.

MAX PULVER'S SYMBOLISM

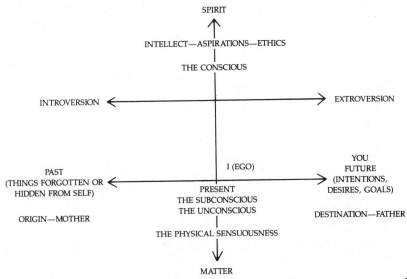

SPIRIT

INTELLECT—ASPIRATIONS—ETHICS

THE CONSCIOUS

INTROVERSION ← → EXTROVERSION

I (EGO)

YOU
FUTURE
(INTENTIONS,
DESIRES, GOALS)

PAST
(THINGS FORGOTTEN OR ← →
HIDDEN FROM SELF)

PRESENT
THE SUBCONSCIOUS
THE UNCONSCIOUS

ORIGIN—MOTHER

DESTINATION—FATHER

THE PHYSICAL SENSUOUSNESS

MATTER

If we were to superimpose a written word with a *t* in it on the spot marked *I (Ego) Present,* and the *t* coincided with the straight up-and-down line, we would be talking about a vertical writer. If the *t* veered to the right, we see from the chart that it would point toward the future. Were it to veer to the left, it would point toward the past. But this same word—say, the word "height"—also reaches into an upper and lower dimension. Upper, middle, and lower areas are called *dimension zones,* and they make up the zonal area.

Think of a child's drawing—a boy standing on a piece of land, the sun shining and some clouds above. Zones are something like that picture. The upper zone represents sky, clouds, the sun—by extension what is high, spiritual, religious, lofty. Conversely, the lower zone represents earth, solidness, what is underfoot—things that are basic, common, earthy, materialistic, sexual. The middle zone is the person, the ego, the *me.*

When handwriting is predominantly in one zone, we see a powerful key to personality. Handwriting confined to the middle zone demonstrates the social person, the today person, the one concerned with Number One and lacking spiritual as well as physical drive.

FIGURE 1.

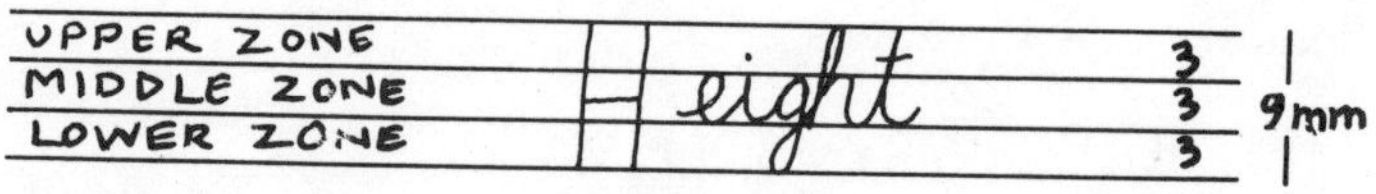

In Figure 1 we see an example of the word "height" laid out on a zonal chart; each zone is 3 millimeters in height, which is the norm.

If the rest of the writing is consistently in the same zones, we say there is balance in this writer. Where the zones fluctuate, the graphologist looks to see what the changes are and analyzes them. If the writer constantly changes the angle of his writing, we see a moody individual, unreliable in his reactions. Where the zones vary, it indicates a shift in motivation.

Take, for instance, the case of a man whose upper-zone writing ordinarily averages three millimeters in height—the norm. Suddenly, the upper zone dwindles to an average of one millimeter. This represents a shifting away from aspirations, spirituality as motivating factors. Usually such a change is accompanied by increased size in one of the other two zones, as if the energy normally expended in the spiritual zone has been shifted to the ego or sexual zones.

Notice the balanced writing, the general equality in the size of the zones in George Washington's script in Figure 2:

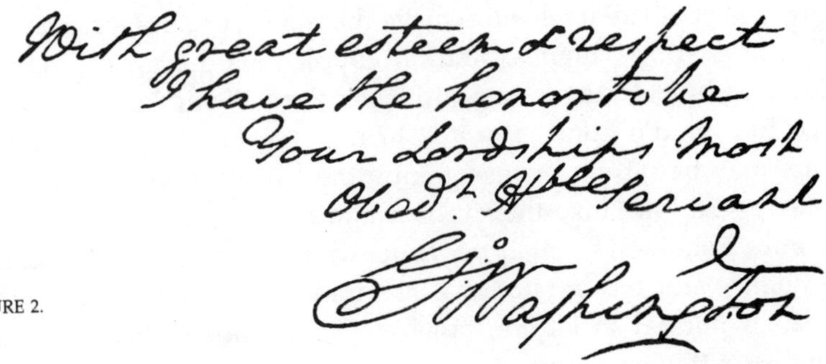

FIGURE 2.

In addition to writing that consistently covers all zones in Figure 1 and writing where there is no consistency whatsoever, we have six other combinations of zonal areas:

FIGURE 3.

FIGURE 4.

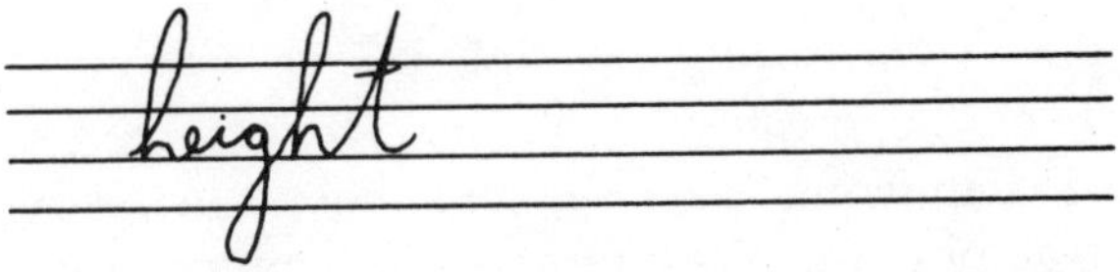

FIGURE 5.

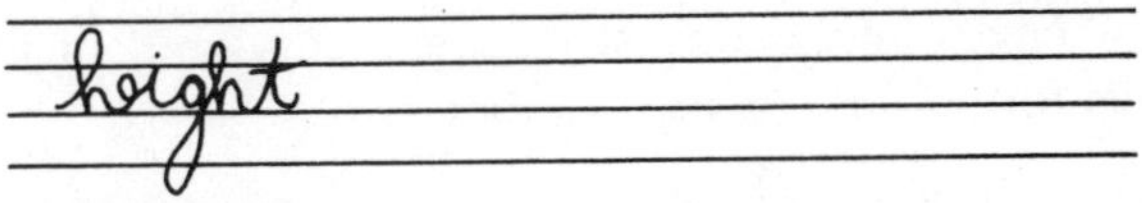

FIGURE 6.

FIGURE 7.

FIGURE 8.

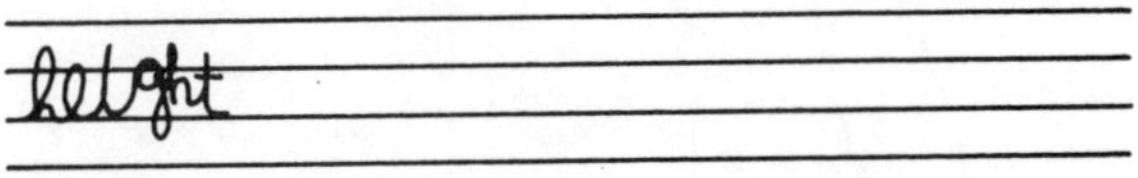

Figure 3 shows the upper zone as the largest. This reveals a person with high aspirations but too little interest in social life, because he has a relatively small lower zone. Although he strives toward high goals, it is doubtful if he will achieve them, because he lacks stamina.

Figure 4 shows high aspiration coupled with physical stamina, evidenced by both the upper and lower zones being large. However, since his middle zone is quite shrunk, his handling of everyday affairs may be off, and consequently the two positive aspects of his character may not take their proper effect.

Figure 5 shows a small upper zone, so the writer probably has little spirituality and few aspirations. His middle zone is average, which reveals a normal social life, but because the accent in this writer's script is on the lower zone, we see someone who is preoccupied with physical pleasures. If the lower zone loop is long and straight down (Figure 5A), it is the sign of sexual pleasure; if the lower zone loop is inflated (Figure 5B), it shows money, materialism.

FIGURE 5A.

FIGURE 5B.

One of the greatest of all heavyweight boxers, the "champion among champions," Jack Dempsey shows by his signature in Figure 5C great physical pleasure and much physical interest. Notice his long, heavy, lower-zone structures—this kind of writing is almost always found among super athletes.

FIGURE 5C.

In Figure 6 we have a large middle zone, a large lower zone, and a small upper zone. This person is a social butterfly. He has strong physical desires, but whether these are material or sexual depends on the shape of the lower zone loop (see Figures 5A and 5B). The small upper zone implies that he has little aspiration.

Figure 7 shows, on the surface, a praiseworthy sort of person— upper zone large (strong aspiration), middle zone large (doing well socially)—but the problem is that there is hardly any lower zone. This is not healthy: the individual needs a proper sexual outlet, and this writer does not seem to have a normal one. Where there is strong sexual repression, sadism, masochism, or other unlovely outlets for desire tend to appear.

In Figure 8, the middle zone predominates. The upper and lower zones are small, showing little spirituality and little desire for material pleasure. The large middle zone hints that social life preoccupies the writer. This is found more often among women than among men, who usually have a small middle zone. In general, women are more interested in social affairs than men are.

A small middle zone, on the other hand, represents strong powers of concentration. People who have small middle-zone letters (*a*, *c*, *e*, and any letter that does not have an upper or lower loop) show great ability at doing work requiring attention to detail. Many scientists, Einstein among them, have very small or even microscopic middle-zone letters. Notice the writing in Polish of Marie Curie:

FIGURE 9.

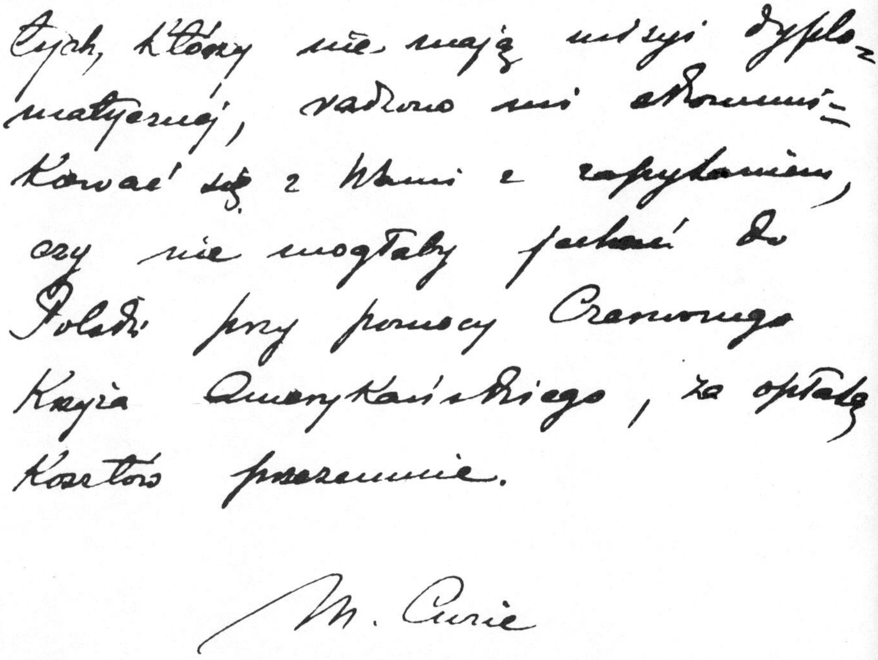

In addition to the tiny middle zone, note the curly Greek *d*'s, showing culture. Some *g*'s and *y*'s are made without return strokes, showing good judgment and mathematical ability. And to top it off, the *t* bars are bowed, showing well-controlled basic instincts, a personality less emotional and more objective than most. Thus, the fine qualities that made this woman a great scientist are plain to read in her handwriting.

4

The *t* Bar

To the graphologist, the two most important letters for analysis are the small *t* and the letter *i*.

In this chapter you will find virtually every possible kind of *t* bar. Any other *t* bar you may come across will probably be only a variation of one of these, and with practice, you should be able to see into which category of *t* bar it fits.

When we speak of the *t* bar, we mean the horizontal line crossing the stem of the *t*. We are not concerned with the letter as a whole.

FIGURE 1.

Figure 1 shows the so-called normal *t*. The *t* bar is perfectly centered, meaning that the length of the bar is equal on both sides of the stem, and the length itself is the normal length. It also crosses the stem in the middle (measuring from top to bottom). This *t* bar shows confidence and self-discipline. It is the kind of *t* we were taught to make as children.

FIGURE 2.

The postplaced *t* bar in Figure 2 is flying away from the stem. Often such writers have quick minds. Their purpose is not exactness in detail; they want to finish quickly. They are aggressive, often showing temper, impatient to reach their goals.

Notice the postplaced *t* bars and postplaced *i* dots of former President John F. Kennedy. Surely a quick mind is indicated.

FIGURE 2A.

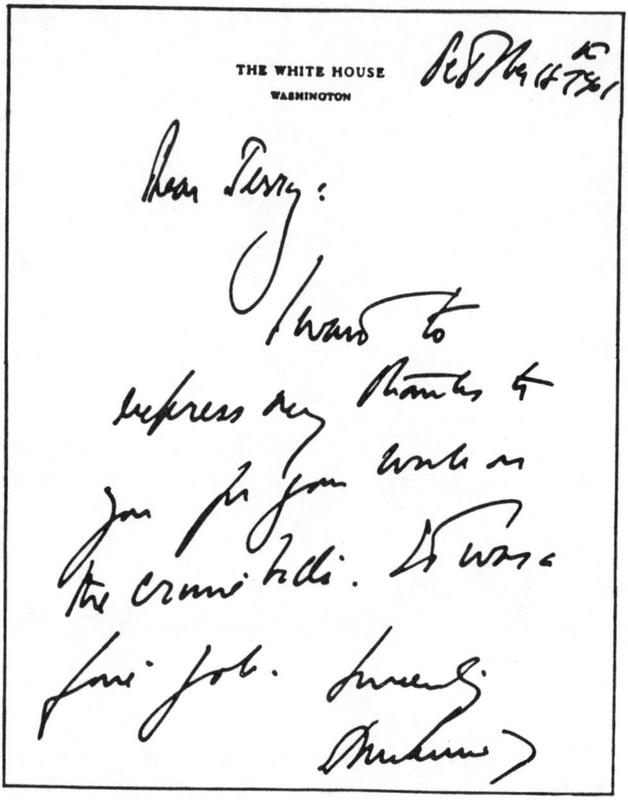

The preplaced *t* bar in Figure 3, besides not crossing the stem, also does not touch it. This writer procrastinates, often shows a lack of self-confidence, and is fearful. It is difficult for him to make decisions. He would rather hold off, as he held off from crossing the stem of the *t*.

FIGURE 3.

The *t* bar in Figure 4 is called a bowed bar (also a convex *t* bar) and is usually found either in the center or the top of the stem. Here it is in the center, showing a strong desire for self-control—like a hand holding back a certain desire the writer wishes to suppress.

FIGURE 4.

FIGURE 5.

In Figure 5, we have the bowed *t* bar at the top of the stem. Since the bar here is in the upper (spiritual) zone, this writer wants to put a curb on his earthy appetites, holding back primitive desires for deep religious reasons.

Observe the bowed *t* bars of Abraham Lincoln:

FIGURE 5A.

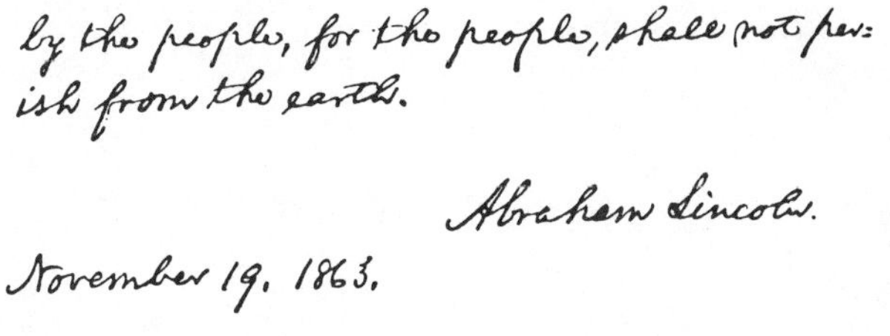

by the people, for the people, shall not perish from the earth.

Abraham Lincoln.

November 19, 1863.

FIGURE 6.

Wherever handwriting produces a knot, as in the knotted *t* bar of Figure 6, it shows persistence, stubbornness, a desire to have one's own way. If, in addition, hooks appear in the letter, like this: , the persistency is accentuated, because the nature of the hook is not to let go.

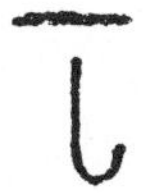

FIGURE 7.

The *t* bar that is above the stem, as in Figure 7, shows the writer to be someone with strong imagination. He is adventurous, he has goals, he is authoritative. If he is able to make his goal a reality, he will probably do so in a great way, for he aims for the stars. (Notice that the *t* bar is in the upper zone). Unfortunately these people are usually unrealistic, so the goals they set for themselves are often unreasonable.

An interesting note: Many graphologists have pointed out that when a person is preoccupied with his occupation, his handwriting will often reveal some kind of symbolism of the tools he uses. This particular *t* bar is commonly found among pilots, as if they thought of themselves as flying.

When one looks at Amelia Earhart's writing, especially her frequent high-flying *t* bars, one easily gets a sensation of flying, of soaring above.

FIGURE 7A.

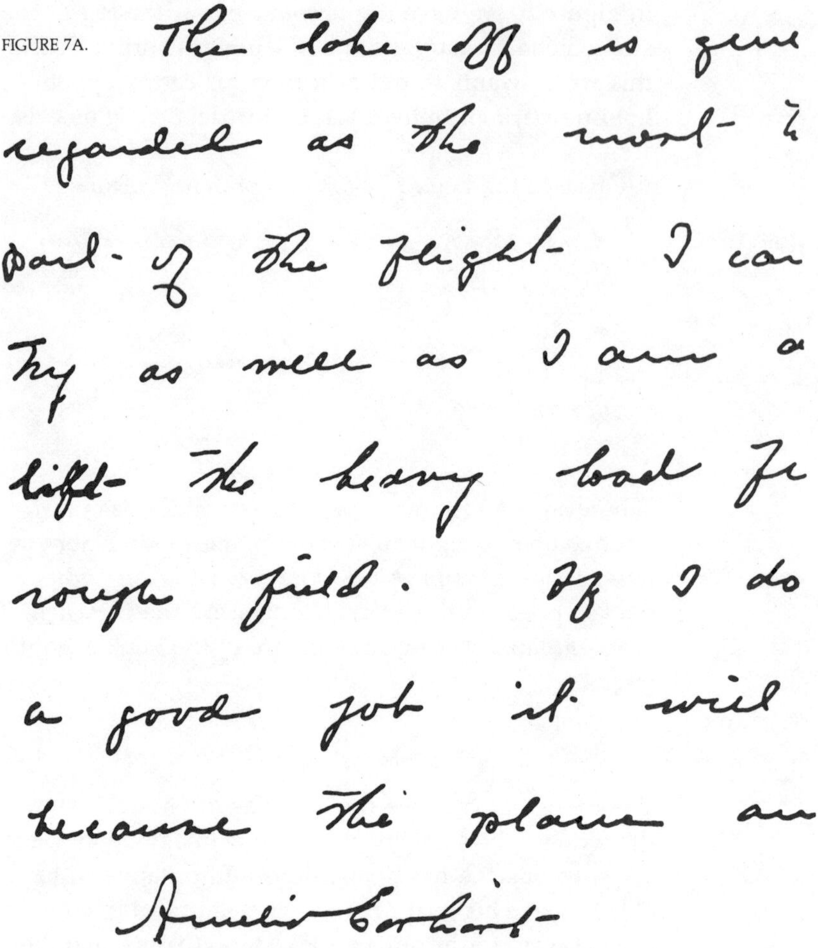

The take-off is gene regarded as the most ? part of the flight. I can Try as well as I am a lift the heavy load ft rough field. If I do a good job it will because the plane an

Amelia Earhart—

Notice the writing of Tony Perkins: Could he have made such a success of Hitchcock's *Psycho* without being adventurous and imaginative? A look at some of his high-flying *t* bars should leave no doubt!

FIGURE 7B.

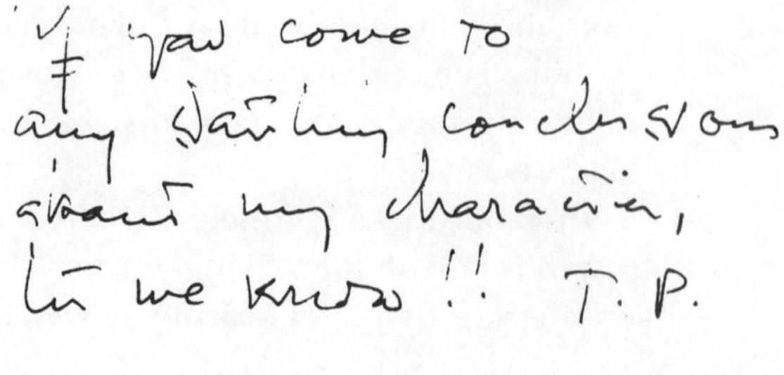

If you come to any darling conclusions about my character, lu we know!! T.P.

FIGURE 8.

Figure 8 is the *t* bar of the rebel, the fighter. Notice the way it is flung down, like a challenge. This writer will not give up; he is a dominant personality, and when he says something, he means it. There is also cruelty in his personality, and he is often sulky, has a low opinion of others, is resentful, and in general is disappointed in life. Even though it is a masculine writing trait, many women write this kind of *t* bar also.

FIGURE 9.

The *t* bar in Figure 9, though it touches the stem, is only half a bar. (It is on the right side of the stem, which represents desires and goals.) There is a certain degree of guilt about the past in this writer—not so severe that it prevents him from touching the stem, but it won't permit him to make a complete bar. (Note: Whenever a *t* bar does not cross the stem, regardless of which side it is located on, it shows repression.)

The *t* stem represents the present. Hence, when the bar appears only to the left of the stem (not shown), it represents some lack on the right, some shortcoming in his goals, his future. When the bar appears only to the right of the stem (as shown), it represents some lack on the left and indicates that the writer prefers not to be in contact with the past, perhaps his childhood.

The *t* bar in Figure 10 shows a person who gives an impression of himself as aggressive. In reality, along with aggression, there is also weakness. The *t* bar descends in a "tough" way, but it does not cross, indicating a certain degree of repression. The writer has guilt feelings, and he lives in the past, as shown by the location of the *t* bar on the left of the stem.

A few of the *t* bars of Richard Speck (Figure 10A), convicted of so many murders, show similar *t* bars in his writing. Also observe the small capital *I*'s, reflecting a severe inferiority complex. (Since the capital *I* reflects the first person in the English language, it shows quite an accurate description, usually done quite subconsciously, of the writer.)

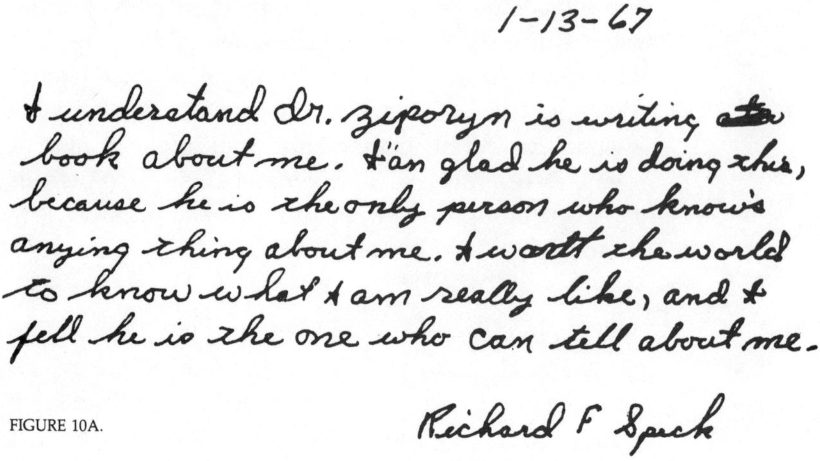

1-13-67

I understand Dr. ziporyn is writing a book about me. I am glad he is doing this, because he is the only person who knows anying thing about me. I want the world to know what I am really like, and I fell he is the one who can tell about me.

Richard F Speck

FIGURE 10A.

FIGURE 11.

Like any *t* bar not crossing the stem, Figure 11 shows a lack of confidence, fears about the self, and, as we mentioned before, repression. In addition, the stem is looped, showing sensitivity—often hypersensitivity. A loop, in general, is blown up to whatever degree necessary for the writer to express his feelings. Loops are signs of vanity. This person is going to be hurt quite often, since he looks for compliments, and is very sensitive.

FIGURE 12.

The concave *t* bar, as in Figure 12, is opposite in shape to the bowed *t* bar and basically opposite in meaning. It shows fickleness, a person who is easily swayed, has weak resistance and weak willpower. The concave-*t*-bar writer takes the easiest way out and prefers not to fight.

FIGURE 13.

A *t* that is not crossed at all, as in Figure 13, may represent many possibilities: carelessness, forgetfulness, physical weakness, bad health, hastiness, impatience—someone who does not have the time to worry about details and wants only to get his thought across. Generally, when the *t* bar is missing, we check for other corroborating signs, such as inclined writing and diminishing size of the middle-zone letters toward the end; if those signs are present, we say the uncrossed *t* bar stands for speed.

FIGURE 14.

The *t* bar in Figure 14 shows hypersensitivity. The writer seems to be so sensitive that he won't even take his hand off the page to cross the stem horizontally (goal-oriented). Instead, without lifting his hand, he scrawls a vertical *t* bar from the bottom of the stem, showing that he lacks strong goals for the future and is sensitive about this area of his life.

FIGURE 15.

Since the *t* bar in Figure 15 is in the form of a knot, it shows persistence. Since the *t* bar is located above the stem, the persistence concerns the self.

FIGURE 16.

The *t* bar in Figure 16 is also in the form of a knot (persistence again), but the fact that the letter is composed of straight lines (forming angles) shows that he will go on to his goals relentlessly.

FIGURE 17.

There are three forms of Figure 17, the long *t* bar, all indicating tenacity and stubbornness.

A.

Figure 17A, a *t* bar with a hook at the left, shows a person who starts out strong but then gives up.

B.

Figure 17B, a *t* bar with a hook at the right, shows someone who may not start out stubborn, but in the process becomes so.

C.

Figure 17C, a *t* bar with hooks at both ends, starts and finishes stubborn, and will fight on to the end of his own course. People like this have a lot of energy and usually move around a lot.

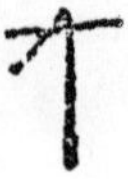

FIGURE 18.

In Figure 18 the *t* bar is placed pretty high on the stem, showing self-confidence. If a *t* bar is located beneath the middle of the stem (t), it shows lack of confidence in the self, as though he did not feel good enough about himself to "stretch up" to his normal height. The fact that the stem descends as it does with such determination shows stubbornness, unwillingness to bend to another's opinion. It is often difficult to get along with such a person; as you can see, he descends to the lower zone to pick up a certain degree of strength.

Note: The height of the *t* bar as an indicator of personality is only relative to what is normal. In some countries students are taught always to cross their *t*'s somewhat lower, or somewhat higher, than is usual with Palmer Method writers. So for them, *relative* height must be borne in mind.

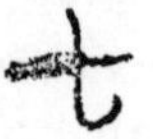

FIGURE 19.

When the *t* bar starts off thick and ends thin, as in Figure 19, it is a sign of one with a sharp tongue and sarcastic personality.

Notice the many pointed, sarcastic *t* bars in the script of Thomas Wolfe:

FIGURE 19A.

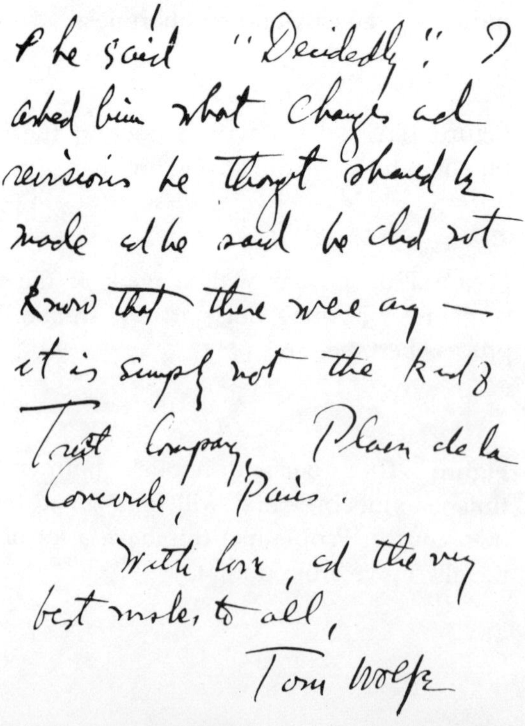

& he said "Decidedly": I
asked him what changes and
revisions he thought should be
made and he said he did not
know that there were any —
it is simply not the kind of
Trust Company, Place de la
Concorde, Paris.
With love, and the very
best wishes to all,
Tom Wolfe

FIGURE 20.

The *t* bar in Figure 20 goes back to the left, representing the past, and thus shows introversion. It also shows jealousy and lack of responsibility, and the hook in the structure of this letter shows greed, egotism, and selfishness.

FIGURE 21.

The *t* bar in Figure 21 crosses in the middle but veers upward. This shows social aspirations and often a strong imagination. (Notice how this *t* bar points to the upper zone.) It is also the sign of one who wants to improve his situation, and is aggressive.

Observe the aggressive and imaginative *t* bars in the writings of both Edith Head (Figure 21A) and Jacqueline Kennedy (Figure 21B). Note also that in both their writings there are other bars that veer in the same direction: the *H* in Miss Head's surname; the capital *I*'s in Jacqueline Kennedy's. Very often these bars will correspond to these *t* bars, as these bars (that is, the bar in the capital *H* and *I*) are written for the same personality reason—the *t* bar is a horizontally written stroke, which is usually written after having taken the writing tool off the paper, the writing also usually being done in a left to right direction. The same physical actions occur with the capital *H* and *I* bars, hence the same direction. In general, these capital *H* and *I* bars (and for that matter, the capital *A* bar) will most often correspond in writing style to how the *t* bars are written, because of the aforementioned reason.

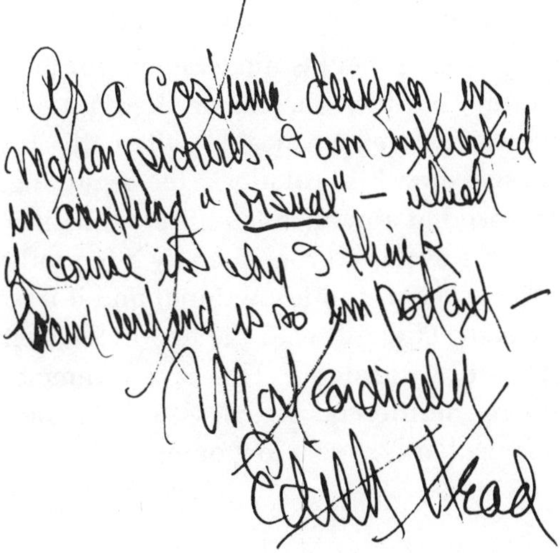

FIGURE 21A.

FIGURE 21B.

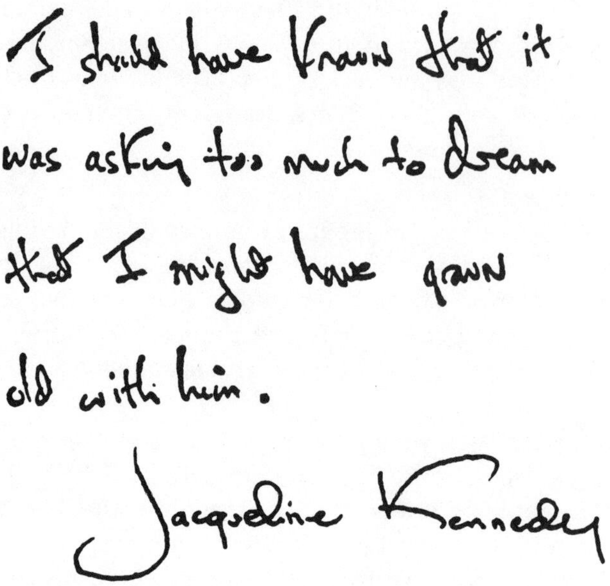

> *I should have known that it*
>
> *was asking too much to dream*
>
> *that I might have grown*
>
> *old with him .*
>
> *Jacqueline Kennedy*

FIGURE 22.

In Figure 22, where only a small part appears to the left of the stem, the *t* bar may look similar to the previous one, but it has a different meaning. This writer is ambitious to the point of having a fighting nature—he looks as if he were holding a bat. He is often the one who would rather take you to court than settle a suit outside.

FIGURE 23.

Figure 23 is writing that reveals a man who can be dangerous. It begins moderately, not too dark, not too muddy, but then the bar on the right side of the stem becomes extremely heavy. Often this type of person doesn't show his brutality in the beginning, but it can be provoked at a moment's notice, without warning.

If this trait is corroborated by other indications in the script, such as muddy writing, and if it is written with the same strength with the bar off the stem (l➘), it may indicate a murderer. This is a common script found among murderers. Needless to say, these writers are resentful and have a low opinion of other people.

FIGURE 24.

A wavy *t* bar, as in Figure 24, is a sign of fun and gaiety, the practical joker mimicking others. It is as if the stroke of the *t* bar were saying, "Ah, don't take me seriously."

FIGURE 25.

The *t* bar with one half of its length scrolled, as in Figure 25, is quite different from the wavy *t* bar. This person, though he answers questions in a more or less straight fashion, does so sarcastically. The straight part of the bar represents his answer to the question, the scrolling represents something of his own which is added on (his sarcasm).

FIGURE 26.

When the *t* stem is looped as in Figure 26, it shows vanity (preening oneself in the presence of others). It also shows prejudice and superficial friendliness, a show-off. This person is bound to make an impression.

FIGURE 27.

This low *t* bar, as in Figure 27, indicates an inferiority complex. The *t* bar by nature shows strength, determination, the will of the individual, self-confidence. Its low placement on the stem shows this writer's lack of self-esteem.

FIGURE 28.

When the *t* bar goes *down* and around and back toward the stem, as in Figure 28, it shows greed, a hoarder. The shape of the arc in the *t* bar looks as if the writer were trying to hold on to something.

FIGURE 29.

When the *t* bar goes *up* and around and points toward the stem, as in Figure 29, this is a sign of egotism. The *t* bar in Figure 28 is really pointing toward the writer's pocket, while that in Figure 29 is pointing toward his own profile.

FIGURE 30.

The *t* bar in Figure 30—which you may or may not recognize as such—shows a person who is quick to lie. The fact that the "bar" starts off as a stem and then converts itself into a bar indicates that the writer did not raise his hand from the paper. If he had let it go at that, it would have shown little else but speed. But the combination of that and the hook implies swiftness plus holding back the truth—he is quick to lie.

Tower

FIGURE 31.

When you have the *t* bar covering the whole word, as in Figure 31, it is a sign of protection, fatherliness. (*Note:* This particular *t* bar is found among many women, often young widows or divorcees. The fact that they are bringing up children alone, having added the fatherly role to that of motherhood, gives us an understanding as to why this "masculine" trait should appear in their handwriting.) If the end stroke comes up and over toward the left (*roof*) it has the same meaning.

Notes about the t *bar and the* i *dot:*

We have seen the relative importance of the *t* bar. There are times when the *t* bar adopts no one stable form throughout a piece of writing. Some *t*'s will have a low-placed bar, others a middle placement, and still others a somewhat high one or even an above-the-stem position. This writing indicates a person who has not yet found his "thing" in life, but is looking.

Generally, every *t* bar has a corresponding *i* dot of the same meaning. The analyzing graphologist keeps a sort of running check and balance between the *t* bars and the *i* dots. To cite two examples: When the writer postplaces the majority of the *t* bars (ʈ), he almost always postplaces the *i* dots too (ʌ˙). Similarly, when the majority of the *t* bars are preplaced (-ʈ), so are the majority of *i* dots (˙ʌ). I use the word "majority" because it is rare for a person to write all his *t* bars or *i* dots the same height or in the same position. The graphologist looks for the overall average.

The *i* dot works in connection with the *t* bar. But the capital *I*, in the English language, has another meaning. When we write the capital *I*, we are visualizing in our minds what we think of ourselves. The *I* stands for the ego, so the special shapes this capital letter takes will show you, in capsule form, the writer's self-image.

If you have wondered why a *t* bar or *i* dot should show the many signs that they do, it is because both represent an additional mark that the writer must stop and make. (The same thing holds true for native writers of languages that are rich in diacriticals, such as the Scandinavian, and their handling implies the same interpretation.) When the writer writes a word containing a *t* or *i*, he must decide whether to cross the *t* bar (or dot the *i*) in the middle of the word, or wait until he finishes the word and then go back. The way he solves this little problem gives an important clue to his individuality.

5

The *i* Dot

FIGURE 1.

The *I* in Figure 1 should be self-explanatory. If this is the image the writer has of himself, surely he is extremely egocentric, a megalomaniac, by virtue of its enormous size.

FIGURE 2.

The *I* in Figure 2 is called a block letter. It shows culture, someone who reads. This is the capital *I* found in most books.

FIGURE 3.

The unadorned *I* of Figure 3 shows nothing extra and similarly indicates the person who sticks to the simplest essentials.

FIGURE 4.

The ugly *I* in Figure 4 is exactly that—ugly. Notice the hook, the sign of egotism and greed. This writer is all out for himself, willing to avoid responsibilities.

FIGURE 5.

The *I* in Figure 5 looks similar to the number 1, thereby showing a relationship to numbers. Often these people are found to excel in mathematics.

Figure 6 is the postplaced *i* dot. This writer's thoughts run in front of his actions, and his writing shows speed. His urge is to finish his task without worrying about exact details.

FIGURE 6.

Figure 7 is the preplaced *i* dot. It shows procrastination, caution, lack of self-confidence, repression. Notice that the *i* dot here is to the left, representing the past (the writer lives in the past), whereas the *i* dot to the right of the stem—the postplaced *i* dot—represents the future.

FIGURE 7.

The *i* dot in Figure 8 is exactly above the stem. This is the sign of accuracy, perfection, excellent judgment, excellent memory, strong adherence to details. This writer often has a matter-of-fact personality. He is not only careful in dotting the *i*, but places it exactly where it belongs. This shows concentration. Many judges and scientists dot their *i*'s in this fashion.

FIGURE 8.

The *i* dots which are exactly above the *i* stem are often found among people who are considered highly moral people. They usually take strongly conservative points of view, in contrast to the writers of the postplaced *i* dots, who are more likely to be liberals. The postplaced writer lets himself go, whereas the exacting writer weighs every action. Notice the many exactly placed *i* dots in Figure 8A (see page 29) of Sigmund Freud's handwriting. He was noted for the meticulousness of his scientific research.

In Figure 9 we have the high-flying dot. This shows the person whose thoughts are high in the sky. He is generally unrealistic, but if he attains his improbable goals, he does so in a big way.

FIGURE 9.

When the *i* dot is not really a dot, but a vertical line, as in Figure 10, it is a sign of criticism, of a person who has a strong concern with principles. Not only does the shape of the dot seem like a descending knife, but it can

FIGURE 10.

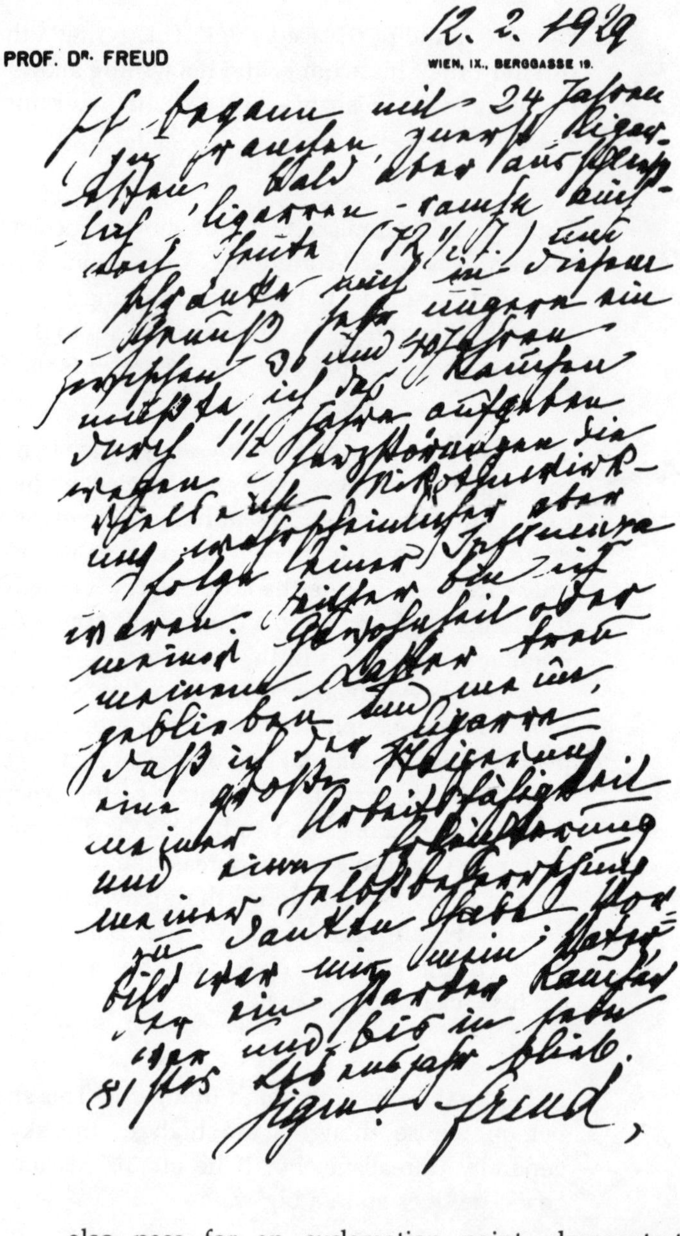

PROF. DR. FREUD

12. 2. 1929

WIEN, IX., BERGGASSE 19.

FIGURE 8A.

also pass for an exclamation point, demonstrating emphasis.

When the *i* dot is in the form of a circle, as in Figure 11, you often find the eccentric—sometimes mildly so,

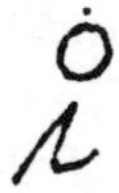
FIGURE 11.

sometimes not so mildly. These people show mild neurotic tendencies and are frequently unable to face reality. They go after fads quite often and are of an artistic nature. The late artist Walt Disney wrote a similar *i* dot. It is interesting that his circled *i* dot looks very similar to Mickey Mouse's round ears.

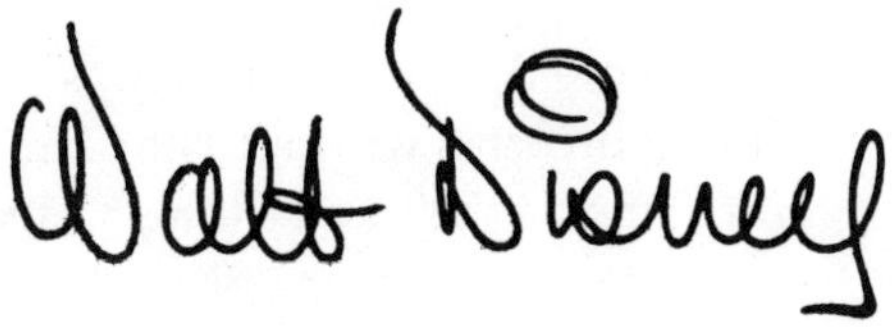

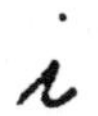
FIGURE 12.

In Figure 12 the *i* dot is very light. This indicates a lack of willpower, possibly physical weakness or even illness, as if the person did not have the strength to dot the *i* properly. (A light *t* bar obviously shows the same meaning.)

The many weak *i* dots and *t* bars of Timothy Leary's writing in Figure 12A indicate physical weakness, perhaps ill health.

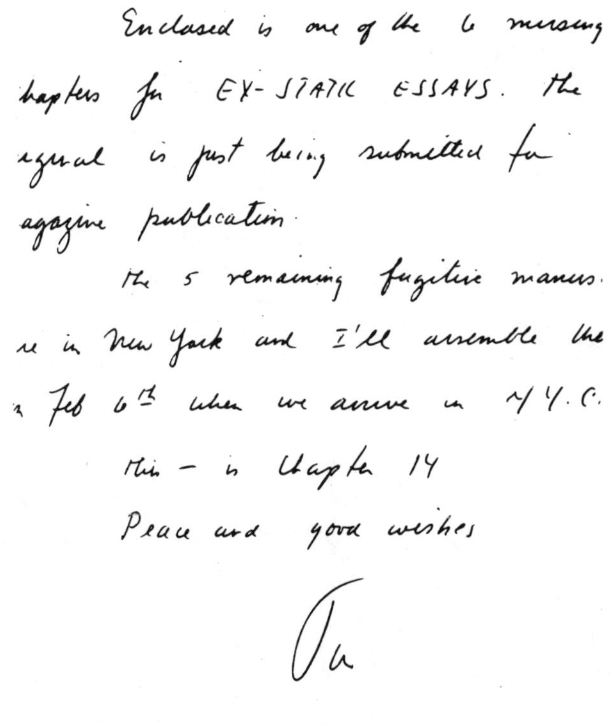
Enclosed is one of the 6 missing
hapters for EX-STATIC ESSAYS. The
iginal is just being submitted for
agazine publication.
The 5 remaining fugitive manus.
re in New York and I'll assemble the
n Feb 6th when we arrive in N.Y.C.
This - is Chapter 14
Peace and good wishes

FIGURE 12A.

FIGURE 13.

When we see an *i* dot joined to another letter (and for that matter, any letter that requires a dot or bar), as in Figure 13, it shows a clever combination of thoughts—doing two things in one shot, so to speak. These are the personalities of chess players, people who can solve abstract and intricate puzzles and make logical deductions.

Observe the clever "hook ups" in Figure 13A of Helen Gurley Brown's writing: The *t* bar with the *h* in "thinks" (fifth line), "the" and "thing" (sixth line):

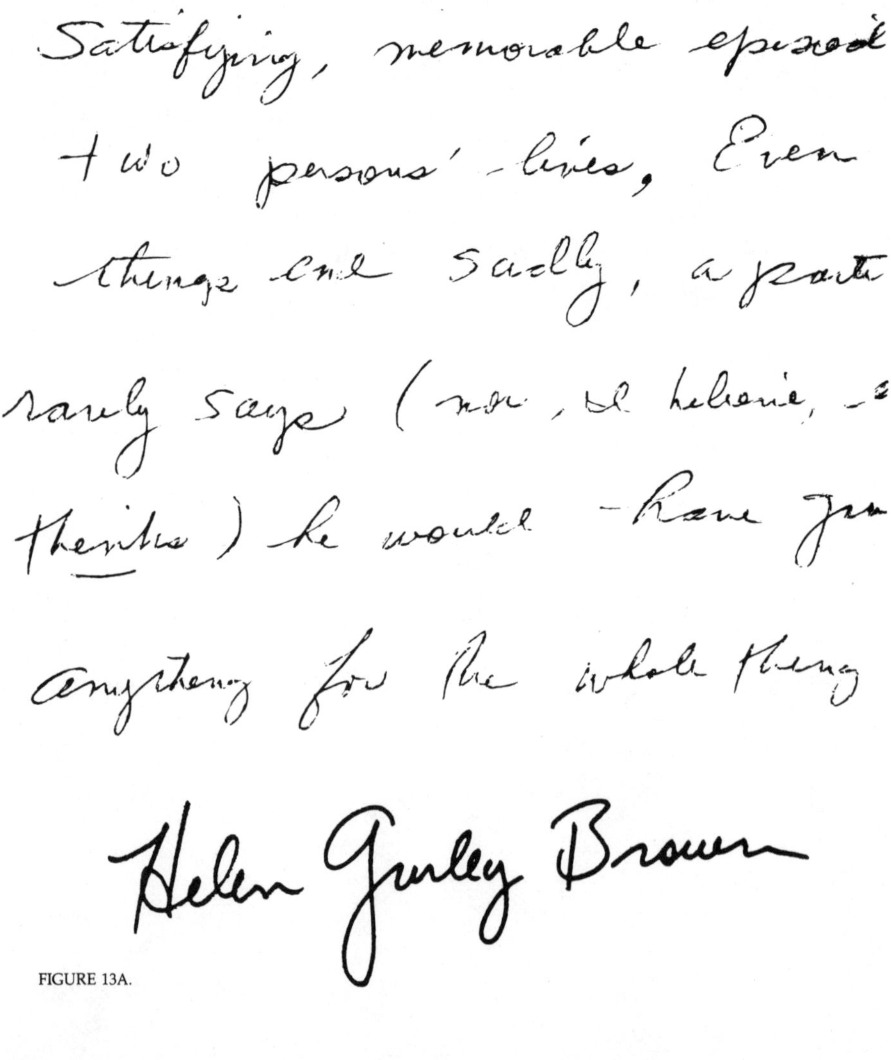

FIGURE 13A.

FIGURE 14.

When the *i* dot is an arc that opens at the left side, as in Figure 14, it is a sign of the neurotic, untrustworthy personality. He shies away from the system. The arc, which is regarded as the eye, is looking toward the left, indicating a lack of trust in somebody he has been involved with in the recent past. (It is often the untrustworthy person who doesn't trust others.)

FIGURE 15.

When the *i* dot is in the form of an arc open to the right, as in Figure 15, it is the sign of the observer. The arc itself looks like an eye staring at something.

FIGURE 16.

When the dot is directly over the stem and heavy, as in Figure 16, it indicates good memory, sound judgment, and the ability to do detail work. You often find this writer to be very materialistic and in a state of depression. (Heaviness in writing shows the physical, and the physical brings on materialism.) Regarding the depression, it seems to be a weight on the writer's head, carrying an extra load.

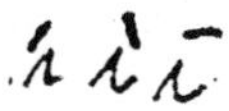

FIGURE 17.

When the dots are more like dashes, as in Figure 17, they signify energy, worry, irritability. If you go over these dots yourself, you can almost feel a liveliness, an irritability, and also a certain degree of speed. When the *i* needs a dot and precision is really necessary, this writer flings his pen in such a manner as to make the dots into dashes. It shows he doesn't care, because there is something bothering him.

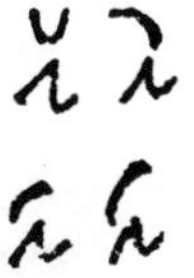

FIGURE 18.

When the *i* dots look more like commas or arcs, as in Figure 18, they are signs of humor, wit, and gaiety. If you look closely at them, they resemble laughing mouths.

FIGURE 19.

An *i* without a dot, as in Figure 19, may simply indicate speed (which would have to be checked with the rest of

the writing). Otherwise the dotless *i* shows forgetfulness, carelessness, neglect. This is also true of the *t* bar
without the bar.

A note about genius: There is no hard-and-fast rule for recognizing
genius through a person's handwriting. However, certain signs often
do appear in the script of great-minded men: high upper-zone
extension (without loops), and/or very small, or even microscopic,
middle zones. (There is no particular guideline to the lower zones.)
Generally speaking, since the middle zone is the social area, the
larger it is, the less the powers of concentration. Thus the great mind
tends to show in his handwriting a willingness to give up the social
world for more intense powers of concentration.

Since the average size of a zone is 3 millimeters, anything under
this size we call small—and the smaller in size it gets, the stronger the
concentration, usually at the expense of sociability. Figure 20, a
specimen of the handwriting of a research scientist, shows this
concentration plainly.

FIGURE 20.

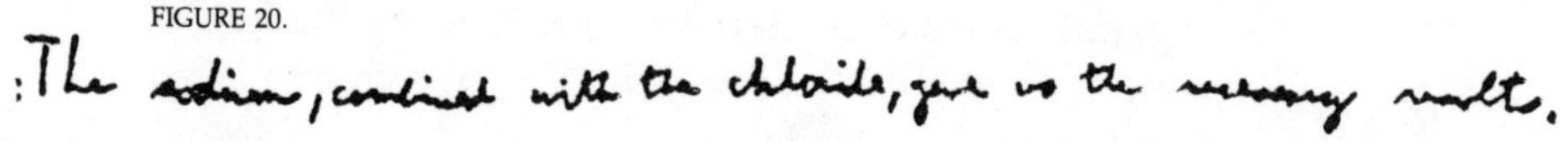

Other traits commonly found in the handwriting of the genius are
tremendous speed and sloppiness, indicating that the person's
thinking is so far ahead of his writing that he has no time for
meticulous penmanship. Figure 21, which was written by another
man engaged in scientific work, displays both qualities.

FIGURE 21.

Although a genius may position many of his *t* bars and *i* dots well to
the right of the stem, he will place others with great precision, for,
however rapidly he may be thinking, much of his work requires
exactitude as well as speed.

A form that frequently turns up in the writing of someone with a
high IQ is a *g* made in the shape of a figure 8, showing speed plus a
certain grace. Figure 22 shows the handwriting sample of a writer:

FIGURE 22.

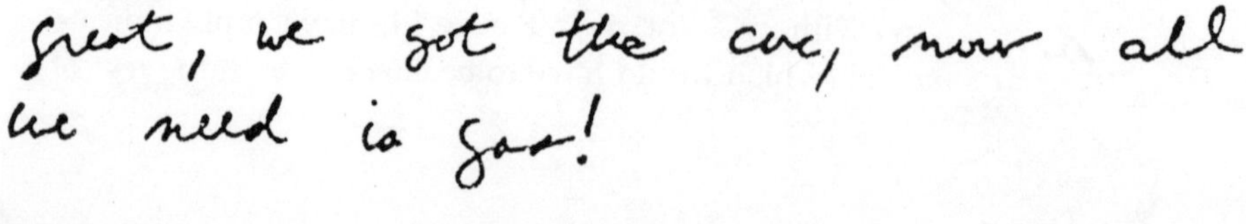

The very quick-minded also frequently link dots or bars of certain letters to the letters before, after, or both (see Chapter 5, Figure 13). This shows a strong ability to combine thoughts and put together ideas which, on the surface, may not appear related at all. Such writers are excellent problem solvers. Notice the writing of Prime Minister Margaret Thatcher of Great Britain (Figure 22A), who cleverly links the *t* bar and the *h* bar in her surname:

FIGURE 22A.

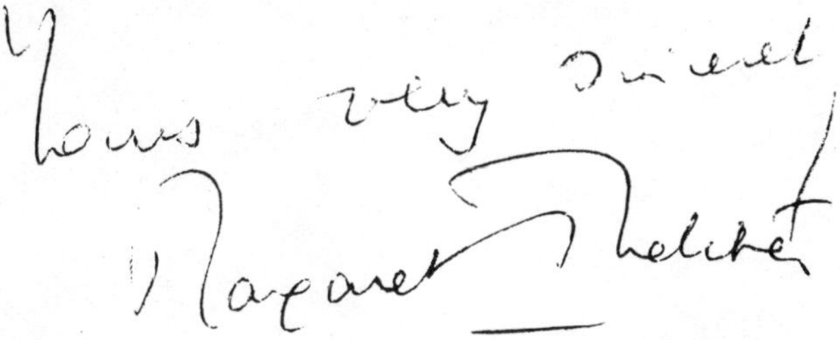

In the following writing we see a speedy hand, showing a quick mind, indicated by the many flyaway *t* bars. Strong aspirations and intellect are shown by the high extensions into the upper zone. Powers of concentration and scientific ability are shown in the small middle zone. The convex *t* bars are indicative of self-control. These excellent personality traits are all present in the handwriting of author-naturalist Charles Darwin, shown in Figure 22B. His writing is so fast that some of the letters are not even completed, as if his mind had more important things to do than to worry about the exact execution of the letters. His *Origin of Species* is still one of the most sought-after books.

FIGURE 22B.

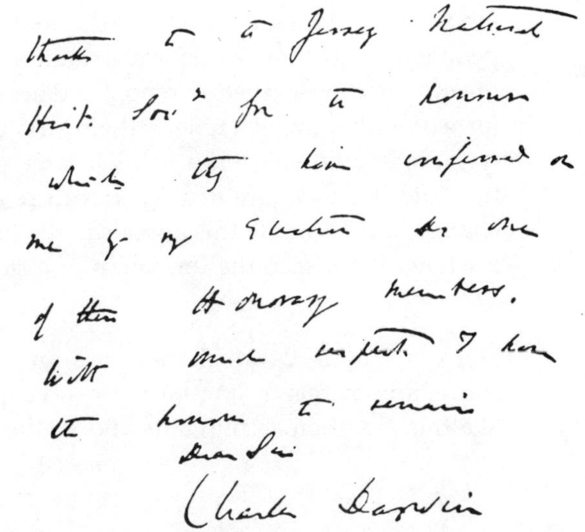

6

Sexuality

Sexuality, of course, plays an important role in our lives. The zone which represents it is the lower zone, and the letter that reveals its quality most effectively is the letter *g*.

Though the letters *f, j, p, q, y,* and *z* also reach into the lower zone, for purposes of exactness graphologists concentrate their analysis on *g* and use the other lower-zone letters for back-up corroboration. Often other letters are useful only in certain specific areas, whereas the writer's method of forming the *g* is always revealing. It is believed that, of the lower-zone looped letters, the *g* most nearly resembles the phallus.

g

FIGURE 1.

Figure 1 shows what we call the Palmer method *g,* the kind we were taught to write in school. Normally, as people mature, they in one way or another drop parts of the system they learned in school and acquire their own form of writing, which reflects their particular personality. People who still write in their later years the way they did in school are usually immature and fearful of change, but naturally this applies to the handwriting as a whole, not just to the formation of a single letter.

q

FIGURE 2.

The *g* in Figure 2, which can pass for the number 9, shows an obvious feeling for figures. People who write like this are often accountants and mathematicians.

36

FIGURE 3.

In Figure 3, we have a *g* similar to that in Figure 2, except that it extends far downward, showing concentration and fatalism. This *g* and the previous one both lack the loops of the Palmer method *g*. As we will see, the upstroke of the *g*: (*upstroke* downstroke) is what we use to measure sexual completion. Since the *g* of Figures 2 and 3 has no upstroke at all (or, as many graphologists call it, a *return* stroke), we see a rejection of sex on the part of the writer.

Concentration is explained in this way: Since materialistic and/or sexual preoccupation can interfere in the thinking process, these factors are here avoided, and the power of concentration is thus freed from being blocked. So in addition to the negative personality we see in this writer, there is also a positive factor.

FIGURE 4.

The *g* in Figure 4 shows avoidance of sexual responsibilities. Where there are open bottoms on ovaled letters (*a p v* etc.,) it shows the embezzler, obviously one who avoids responsibility. Since this open oval is at the bottom of a "sexual" letter, we see avoidance of sexual responsibility. As written here, this open oval can be viewed as a circle which is lacking something—the same part which is lacking in this writer's personality.

FIGURE 5.

When the upstroke does not go through the downstroke, as in the various *g*'s of Figure 5, it is a sign of masturbation or of virginity, a sign of no really strong sexual fixation.

FIGURE 5A.

If you will measure the downstroke of the *g* in Figure 5A, you will see it measures 8 millimeters, whereas the upstroke measures only 2 millimeters. The downstroke indicates the amount of sexual strength in the writer, the upstroke, how much of the downstroke is being completed. Here the gap is tremendous. The writer is very sexually incomplete, considering the amount of energy he is putting out as compared to the amount he is taking in.

FIGURE 5B.

When the upstroke crosses the downstroke, as in Figure 5B, it shows completion—to a certain extent. However, since the downstroke is larger than the upstroke, it shows a gap in the completion—therefore, frustration.

As a rule of thumb, since the *g* is supposed to be in two zones (middle and lower) and each zone's normal size is 3 millimeters, the part of the *g* in the lower zone should measure an average of 3 millimeters for the downstroke as well as for the upstroke. When the downstroke measures *more* than the upstroke, regardless of whether it *crosses* the upstroke or not, the amount of frustration can be measured by the difference.

If, for example, the downstroke measures 5 millimeters—2 millimeters longer than the "normal" downstroke—then the upstroke should measure 5 millimeters, too. A "normal" 3-millimeter upstroke would represent 2 millimeters of frustration.

FIGURE 6.

The *g* in Figure 6 shows a closed triangle, and indicates someone who can be a tyrant in his own home, usually because of sexual disappointment. All angles hint at rigidity. When these angles are found in the lower zone, they show that the writer's rigidity is caused by what the area represents, the sexuality.

Graphologists refer to this *g* structure as the "henpecker." Whenever a triangular shape appears in the lower zone, it probably means argumentativeness, bickering, et cetera. Whenever a triangle appears, as is the case here, with the point at the bottom, we see the writer, whether male or female, as having a strong interest in the female body. When this sign appears in a woman's writing, it does not necessarily mean that she is a lesbian, for many clothing models and women in the fashion field write like this. It simply implies a preoccupation with the female figure. However, many lesbians do write *g*'s with downward-pointing loops, and some women write phallic symbols along with the triangular (female) loops, showing bisexuality.

FIGURE 7.

The *g* in Figure 7 shows a double loop, which is found among people with strange habits. It is associated with drug usage, and it shows confusion, perhaps a drive so strong that the writer has succumbed to it. Although many physical drives are difficult to control, this one is doubly so.

FIGURE 8.

The form in Figure 8 is supposed to be a *g*. The down- and upstrokes of this figure are so distorted that they probably represent the sex pervert.

FIGURE 9.

An extremely large loop, as in Figure 9, shows a tremendous sexual imagination. It resembles the phallus, and since the lower zone reflects the sexuality of the individual, its size indicates that sex dominates the writer's thinking.

Notice the large underlength in Jayne Mansfield's capital letter of her first name in Figure 9A.

FIGURE 9A.

FIGURE 10.

The loop shown in Figure 10, though similar to that in Figure 9 and showing strong sexuality, actually stresses materialism.

FIGURE 11.

When the *g* loop is sharp at the bottom, as in Figure 11, we see a piercing, penetrating one who does not give up easily, one who wants his own way. This writer will also be revengeful. He takes a hardened, rigid approach to sex, as is indicated by the sharpness of the angles. (Notice how the shape resembles a knife blade.)

FIGURE 12.

The flimsy-looking *g* in Figure 12 shows a person who is weak and/or shy sexually. A certain amount of physical strength is necessary for normal relations. This writer is lacking in this area, as reflected by the feebleness of the loop, which is an indicator of the physical (sexual) strength of the individual.

FIGURE 13.

The *g* in Figure 13 has a triangle loop, its base being horizontal. The fact that it is large in the lower zone shows materialism, and the fact that it is set on a base shows that the writer needs a solid basis for this materialism.

Figure 13 bears a superficial resemblance to Figure 6, but they mean different things graphologically. In Figure 6 the point is at the bottom, reflecting an interest in the female form. Here the bottom is flat, horizontal.

FIGURE 14.

The *g* in Figure 14 is in the form of an open 8, a trait often found among lesbians. If you turn the figure onto its side, you will see a pair of breasts. The female form is on the mind of this female writer.

FIGURE 15.

The loop in Figure 15 comes up and around, pointing back to the left (the self). The underlength is inflated, showing materialism, and that, combined with the self-pointing loop, adds up to greed and egotism.

The writing in Figure 16 shows hypersexuality. This person lives for pleasure, regardless of what may come of it, as we see by the way in which the loops have entangled themselves.

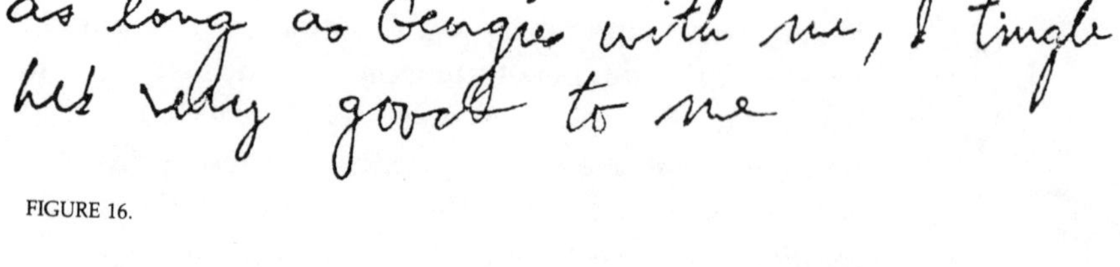

as long as Georgie with me, I tingle his very good to me

FIGURE 16.

FIGURE 16A.

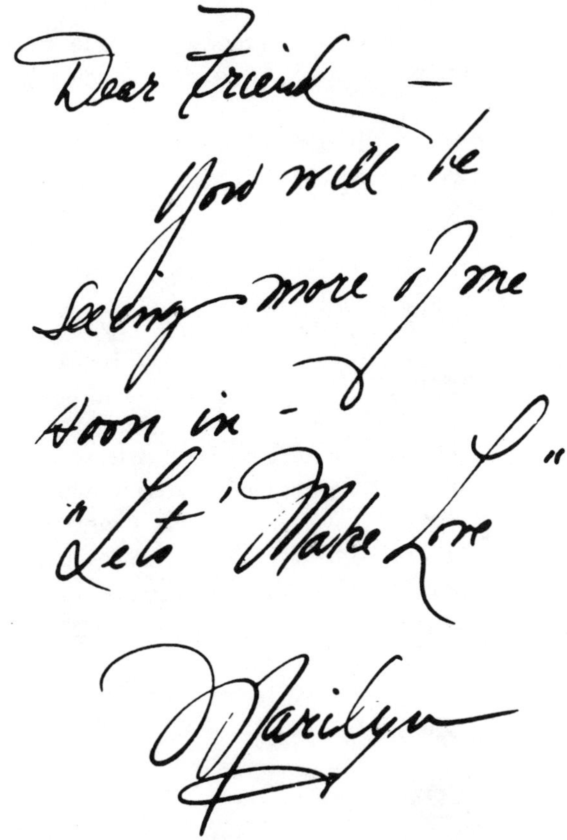

The spacing between the lines in Marilyn Monroe's writing is quite large and still the underlength loop in "you" chokes into the line below it.

FIGURE 17.

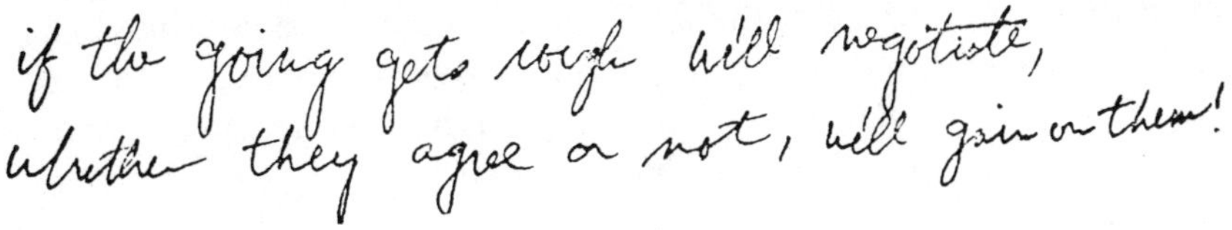

The example in Figure 17 shows strong sexuality, though not as much as the previous one. The loops here are quite large, though not nearly as large as those found in the previous example, and they are not entangled in other letters.

The example in Figure 18 shows moderate sexuality. This writer is able to keep control over himself, as sex plays a role among the other roles in his life.

As a rule of thumb, if the lower zone is either equal or smaller in size to the upper zone, the sexual drive will be under control.

FIGURE 18.

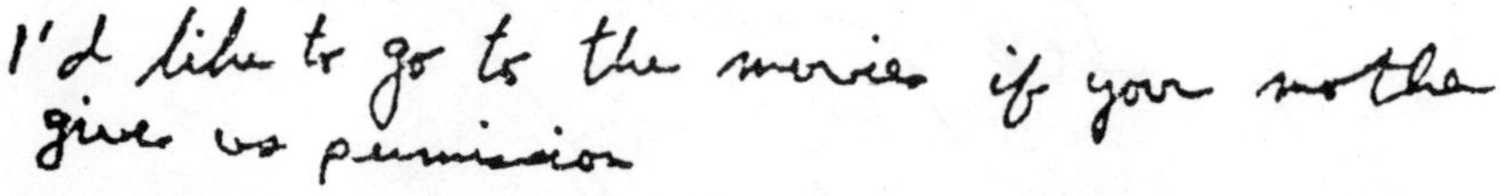

I'd like to go to the movies if your mother gives us permission

The example in Figure 19 shows a person who is undersexed. His situation is not a healthy one. He has aborted natural sexual energy, and it would be advisable for him to get counseling. When the underlengths are as short as they are here, we see a person who, if he is not a physical weakling, lacks drive and sexual strength, one who becomes weary easily.

FIGURE 19.

whatever daddy and mommy tell me I'll listen, 'cause they're right

The example in Figure 20 shows two things which we are concerned about. We see that the upstroke and downstroke both meet at the point where the downstroke begins—this being just under the oval part of the *g*. We also see that the same basic amount of strength is used in the upstrokes as in the downstrokes (we call this even-pressured). Usually the downstroke is a bit heavier, but that doesn't matter as long as there are no marked differences. Here we have a writer who started and finished with the same basic amount of sexual strength—a healthy sex life.

FIGURE 20.

I get a lot of get up and go

The example in Figure 21 has both positive and negative factors. The upstroke does cross the downstroke—but either somewhere in the middle or toward the bottom. Though the writer does complete the act, he probably has orgasm before his partner, which often leads to frustration in the relationship. There is a selfishness in this writer's makeup, since he lacks consideration for his partner.

FIGURE 21.

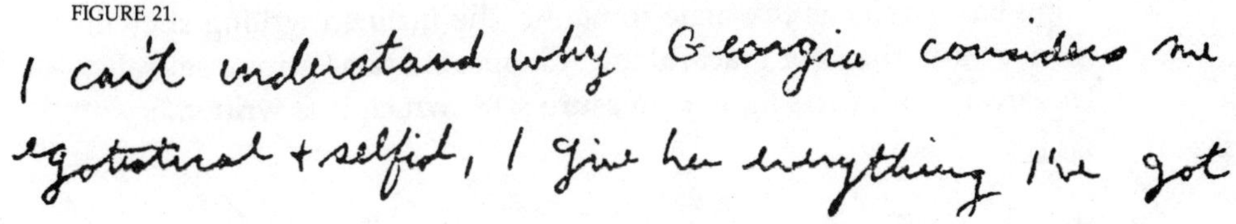

I can't understand why Georgia considers me egotistical + selfish, I give her everything I've got

The example in Figure 22 shows the downstroke having much more pressure than the upstroke, though the upstrokes do cross the downstrokes at the "proper" place. This trait shows that whatever strength the writer has is used in the beginning, but he somehow manages to complete the act.

FIGURE 22.

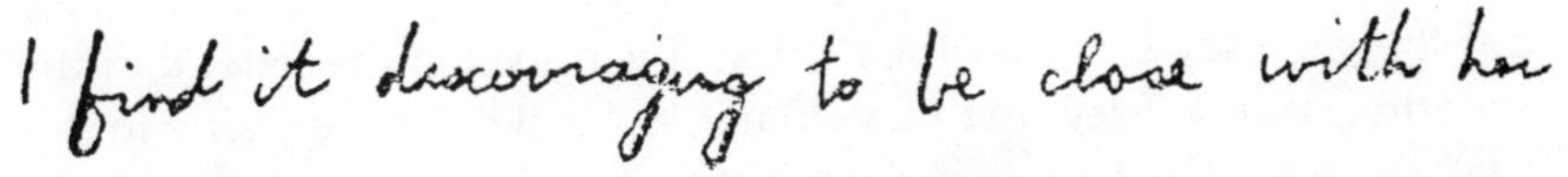

I find it discouraging to be close with her

The upstroke in Figure 23 is hardly an upstroke at all. The action was started, but it wasn't finished. Or perhaps the person does often "finish" with masturbation.

FIGURE 23.

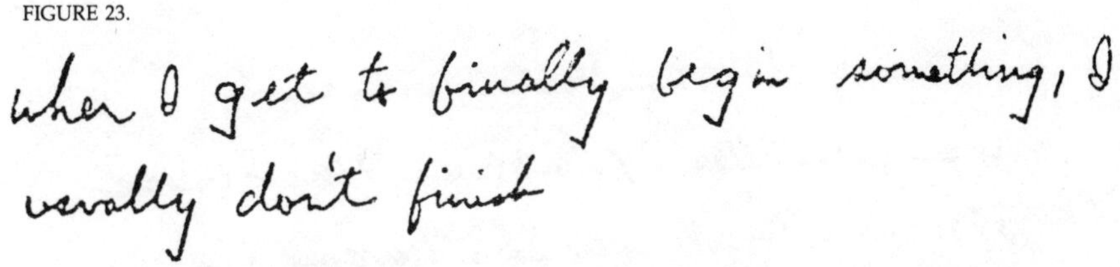

when I get to finally begin something, I usually don't finish

The example in Figure 24 is the writing of a man who is a romantic. His writing leans to the right, showing warmth, and his long lower loops indicate strong sexual feeling. We generally find a man writes with heavier pressure than a woman does. Compare this with the female counterpart in the following example.

FIGURE 24.

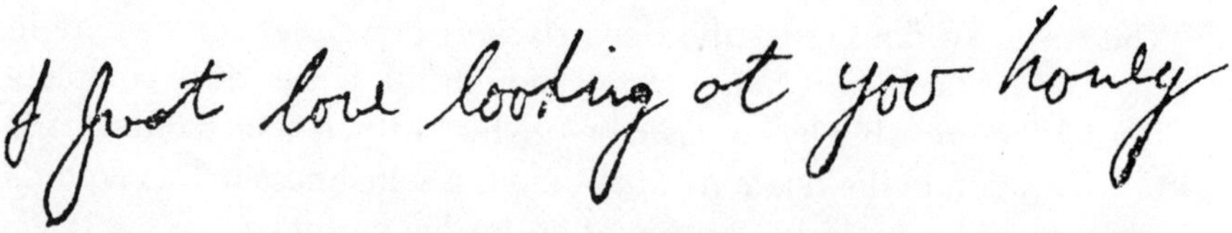

I just love looking at you honey

In Figure 25 we have the woman who is quite romantic. She has the same basic traits as the male romantic: the inclined writing showing the warmth; the long graceful lower loops, showing strong sexuality. However, notice the lighter pressure with which it is written.

FIGURE 25.

living with you means everything to me

FIGURE 26.

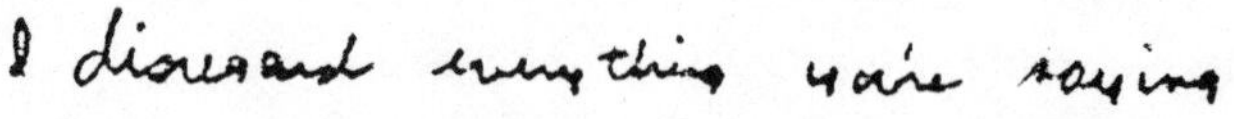

I disregard everything you're saying

The above writing shows the writing of a sadist. If you look closely at the *g*'s, they can pass for *a*'s, but if you look at the letter *a* in the writing, you will see that they do not look alike. The sexuality in this person has gone haywire. There's no natural outlet (as indicated by having virtually no underlengths) so the writer gets his pleasure from unhealthy forms of expression, such as inflicting pain. The Marquis de Sade (from whom we got the term "sadist") wrote similarly (*See* Figure 26A.)

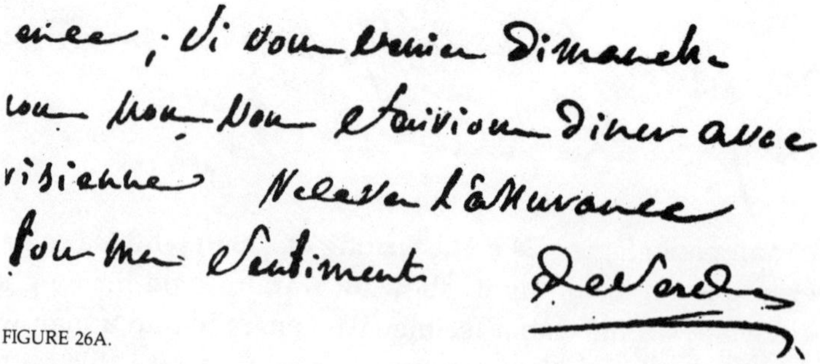

FIGURE 26A.

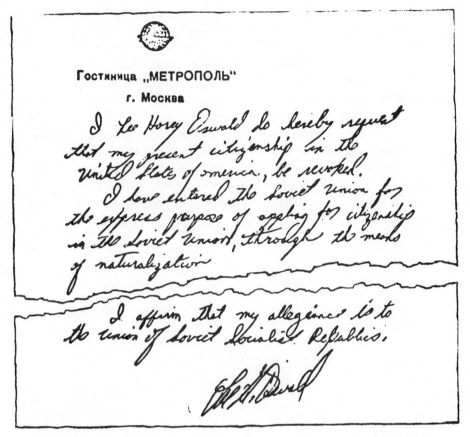

Гостиница „МЕТРОПОЛЬ"

г. Москва

I Lee Harey Oswald do hereby request that my present citizenship in the United States of America, be revoked.

I have entered the Soviet Union for the express purpose of appling for citizenship in the Soviet Union, through the means of naturalization

I affirm that my allegiance is to the union of Soviet Socialist Republics.

FIGURE 26B.

The writing in Figure 27 is clearly inclined, showing a dependency on others. The writing is also extremely smeary, as if an ink blotter were used on it. This writing is called *pastose*—a term from the field of printing, meaning "covered with thick paint"—and it shows very strong sensuousness.

The inclined writing here, in obvious comparison to Figure 26, shows obedience, as if the writer were humbling himself—but for the sole purpose of deriving benefit therefrom. This is the handwriting of

FIGURE 27.

I need to be punished, it's the only way out for me, I sure it will do wonders for me

a masochist. Leopold von Sacher-Masoch (from whose name is derived the term "masochist") wrote similarly.

Whenever there is extremely pastose writing, we are dealing with a sensually abnormal individual. Notice the similarities in the writings of the Marquis de Sade (Figure 26A) and Lee Harvey Oswald, President Kennedy's assassin (Figure 26B). Both are excessively muddy and ink-filled, which indicates sensuality. De Sade's writing also contains piercing end strokes, and since the end strokes represent his relationship to his fellowman, this indicates the pleasure he took in cruelty. Oswald's writing also has many angles and hooks, showing a rigid, pigheaded approach. Rigidity, coupled with abnormal sensuality, can trigger the possessor into a most barbaric act.

The Base Line

In handwriting analysis, the base line—how straight the subject writes—reflects mood. In order to ensure that the base line is accurately read, it is best that the paper be unlined, for lined paper has a way of guiding the writer in a course which may not be his real self.

FIGURE 1.

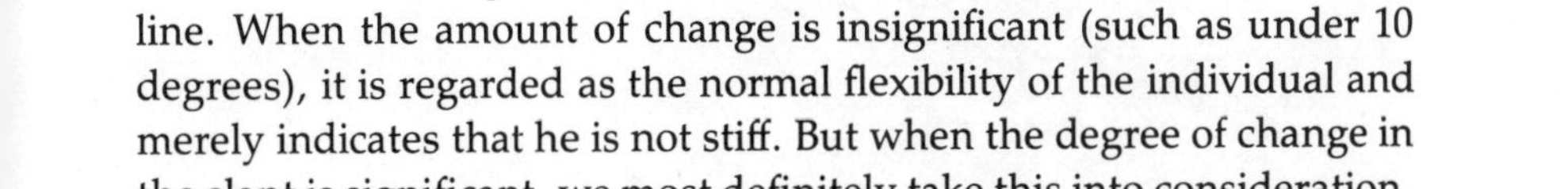

I've been working from 9-5 for forty years now

Most writing has some degree of variation. The variations often occur in the writing slant and also, but not as frequently, in the base line. When the amount of change is insignificant (such as under 10 degrees), it is regarded as the normal flexibility of the individual and merely indicates that he is not stiff. But when the degree of change in the slant is significant, we most definitely take this into consideration.

The writing in Figure 1 is more or less straight. You can see this by taking a ruler and placing it under the middle-zone letters—they are all basically equidistant from the ruler. Generally speaking, when the base line is straight (and certain other factors are not present), we find an individual who doesn't go to pieces if something unexpected occurs. He is composed, not easily upset, straight thinking, and honest.

Observe the straight base line of Thomas Jefferson's writing in Figure 1A, showing honesty:

FIGURE 1A.

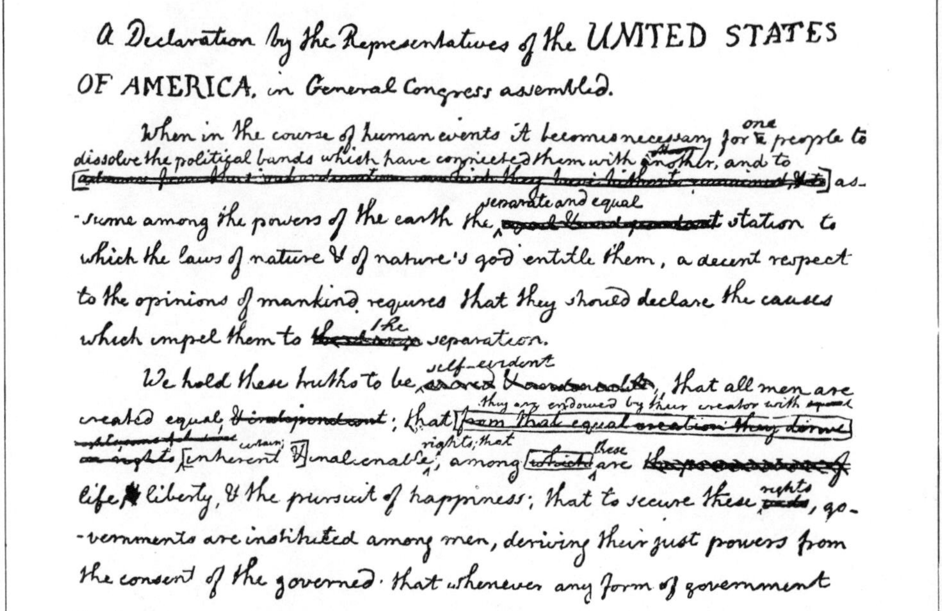

A Declaration by the Representatives of the UNITED STATES OF AMERICA, in General Congress assembled.

When in the course of human events it becomes necessary for one people to dissolve the political bands which have connected them with another, and to assume among the powers of the earth the separate and equal station to which the laws of nature & of nature's god entitle them, a decent respect to the opinions of mankind requires that they should declare the causes which impel them to the separation.

We hold these truths to be self-evident, that all men are created equal; that they are endowed by their creator with [inherent &] unalienable rights; that among these are life, liberty, & the pursuit of happiness; that to secure these rights, governments are instituted among men, deriving their just powers from the consent of the governed; that whenever any form of government

THE FIRST DRAFT OF THE DECLARATION OF INDEPENDENCE IN JEFFERSON'S HANDWRITING, AND WITH HIS OWN CORRECTIONS.

(*From the original, preserved in Washington.*)

FIGURE 2.

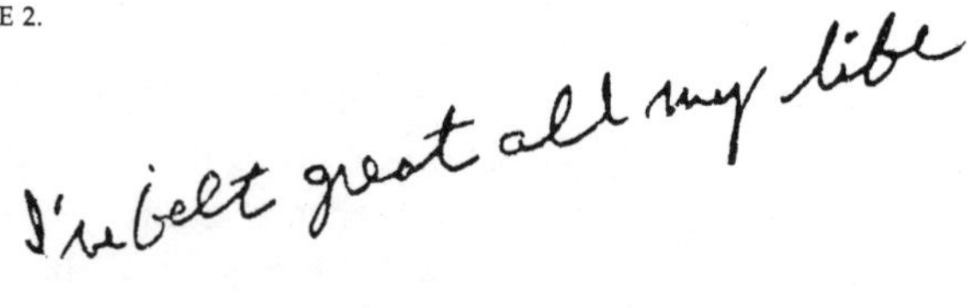

The writing in Figure 2 has what is called an *ascending base line,* climbing toward the sky. This is the writing of an optimist. People who write like this are not easily discouraged and are a delight to have around, since they usually look on the bright side of life. There is a problem with them, however; often they do not look at facts too closely, because of their optimistic personalities, and this obviously impairs their judgment.

As the base line begins ascending, we see the degree of optimism: the higher the ascent, the higher the degree of optimism—along with a higher degree of impracticality.

Star of television's *Starsky and Hutch*, David Soul, has quite an ascending handwriting, showing him to be quite optimistic and not easily discouraged.

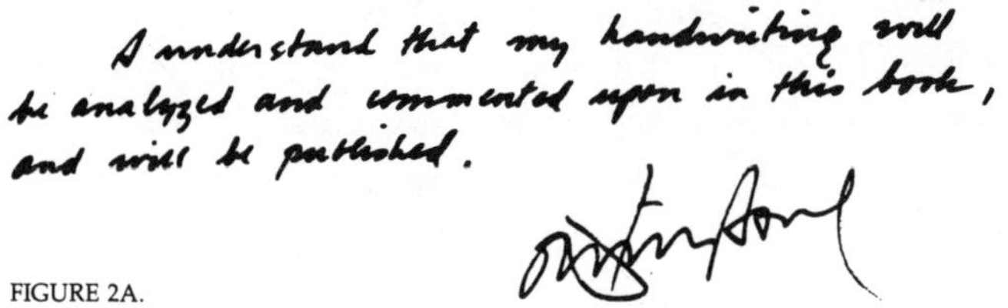

FIGURE 2A.

Though not raised to the same degree, look at John Wayne's raised base line in Figure 2B. Coupled with those long *t* bars, the Duke shows optimism and aggressiveness in his forceful script.

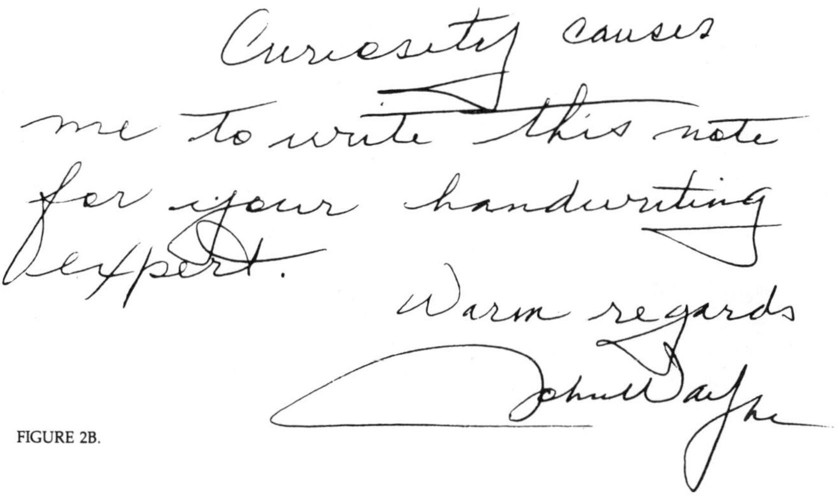

FIGURE 2B.

The example in Figure 3 is the writing of a pessimist, called a *descending base line*. This person is always down. The deeper his base line descends, the deeper the pessimism. Also, the more angular the letters are, the more confirmed his pessimism.

FIGURE 3.

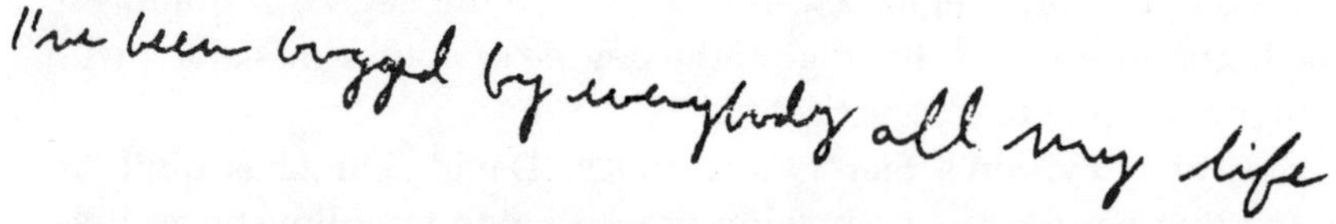

I've been bragged by everybody all my life

If you ever wonder why, when you make a suggestion to a group of people, there is one man who never wants to risk it, take a good look at his handwriting. If you see a descending base line, you will know that by nature he lacks enthusiasm for new plans or ideas, feeling that none of them will work out anyway. His criticism is not necessarily directed at your suggestion; he is, in general, a skeptic and will probably shoot down everybody's ideas.

Notice two signatures of Napoleon:

FIGURE 4A.   FIGURE 4B.

Figure 4A was made at the time of his triumph. The signature shows an extremely ascending writing, properly reflecting his state of elation. Figure 4B was made at the time of his abdication, and its downward, fallen fashion reflects his state of depression.

FIGURE 5.

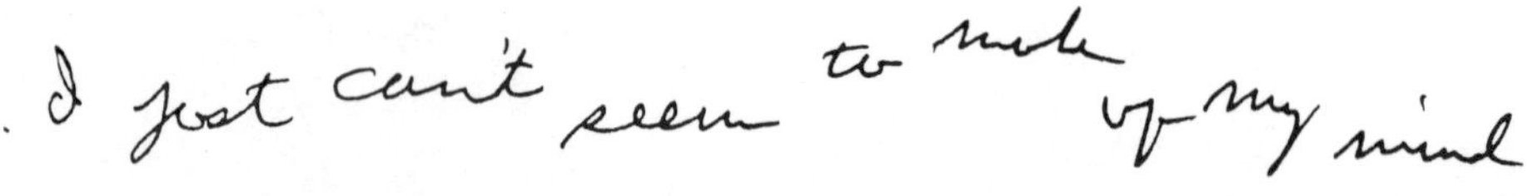

I just can't seem to make up my mind

The bobbing and weaving example in Figure 5 is called the *varying base line*. There is no real way of predicting this writer's next move. He is inconsistent, prey to mood swings. It is difficult for him to hold a job or perform any function requiring steadiness. Others will have difficulty getting along with him, for one moment he is ambitious and aggressive, and the next depressed.

The mood of the writer reflects a great deal of his total personality, so the base line is quite important for purposes of analysis. But it is useful for the graphologist to have samples of the subject's writing done at different times, so that the variations in it can be taken into consideration.

8

The Margins

The margin shows how the writer spends his money and his attitude toward handling friends. In Figure 1, we see a small left margin and a wide right margin. This person is a real spender. He probably begins with a budget of some type, but his true nature soon gets the better of him. The left shows where he begins and the right shows where he is going. Since the right margin is left blank (and the right, as we know, represents the future) we see that he avoids thinking about the future and probably has a fear of it.

FIGURE 1.

Figure 2 is the opposite of Figure 1. This writer starts as a generous spender and ends pinching pennies as indicated by the cramped right margin. His blank left-hand margin also indicates a fear of the past.

FIGURE 2.

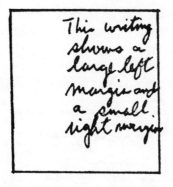

The margin in Figure 3 starts off narrow but as it proceeds down the page, it widens. He begins with a budget, but is unable to maintain one. His true nature is to spend. Interestingly enough, on the following page, this writer will once again begin narrow and end wide.

FIGURE 3.

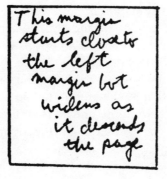

The writing in Figure 4 shows that the individual wants to be generous—at least, that is the impression he would like to give. He may be sincere about donating, but eventually, his real self (being thrifty) wins out, and he ends up counting pennies. This is shown by the left margin beginning quite wide and ending almost nonexistent.

FIGURE 4.

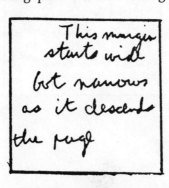

The margins in Figure 5 have no particular order. This writer may indulge in excessive spending and then suddenly go on a budget. He has no set order as far as finances are concerned. When he has money, he spends—when he doesn't, he does not take it to heart. To him, money is only a means, and he manages quite well without it.

FIGURE 5.

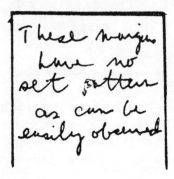

Figure 6 shows a small margin at both sides. This indicates that the writer uses accurate judgment and thrift when shopping. A small margin or no margin at all shows a person who is careful of every penny. Sometimes, in making certain that he is not overcharged, he outwits himself and misses out on a genuine bargain.

The top margin—that is, the area at the top of the page—indicates the writer's attitude toward the one he is writing to. The more space left blank, the more respect he feels. If the top margin, reflecting the upper (spiritual) zone is wide, it shows awe for the addressee (the writer does not wish to tread in the spiritual zone). If the top margin is completely filled, it indicates a general lack of respect.

FIGURE 6.

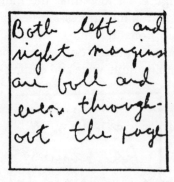

The lower margin—the bottom of the page—is negligible in meaning. However, if someone writes consistently at the bottom of many pages, it usually indicates depression—especially if the signature sags to the bottom. The fact that he writes at the down part of the pages represents his state of mind.

9

Beginning and End Strokes

When someone starts to write a letter, he must immediately decide where and how he should form it. In school, we were taught to start with a soft curving loop and end the same way. This was the Palmer Method. As the writer matures, he usually drops the beginning strokes or develops an individualized beginning stroke, different from what he was taught in school. If he does not, his writing will usually be classed as immature.

FIGURE 1.

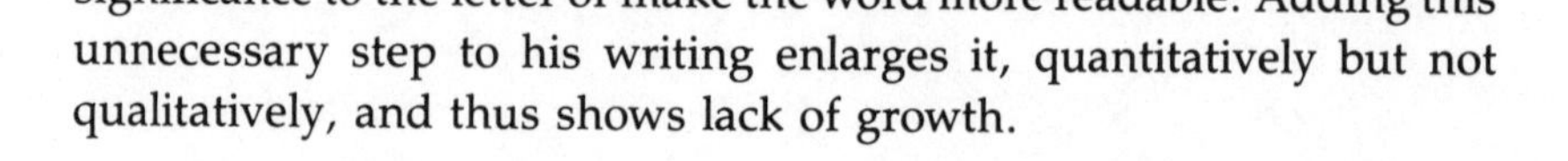

The copybook writing in Figure 1 shows immaturity. This writer still adheres to the use of beginning strokes, which do not add any significance to the letter or make the word more readable. Adding this unnecessary step to his writing enlarges it, quantitatively but not qualitatively, and thus shows lack of growth.

FIGURE 2.

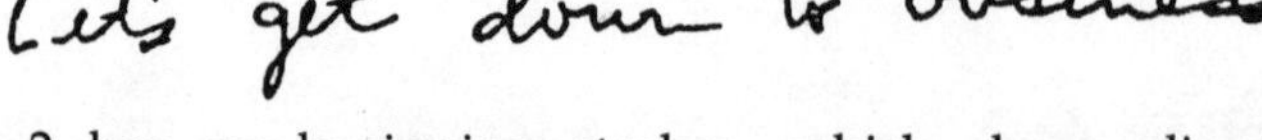

Figure 2 has no beginning strokes, which shows directness, someone who gets right down to the point without commotion. It is the handwriting of the mature individual.

Notice that there isn't even one word in Salvadore Dali's writing in Figure 2A that contains a beginning stroke. He surely gets right down to business. The many knotted *t* bars show him to be a diligent worker as well.

FIGURE 2A.

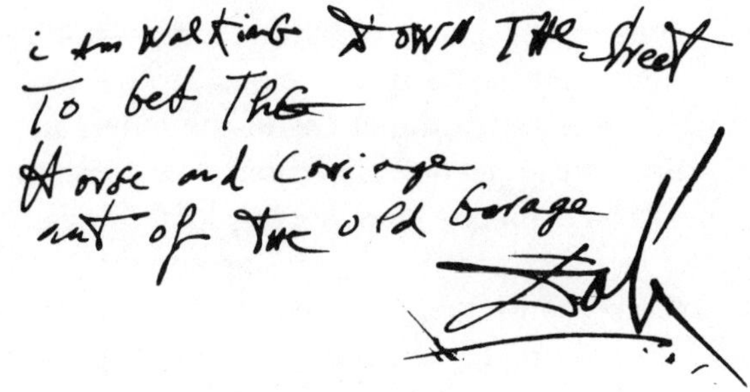

i am walking down the street
to get the
Horse and Coriage
out of the old Garage

FIGURE 3.

cits call cmine

Figure 3 shows hooks that are inturned (so much so that at first glance they appear to be *c*'s). This reveals selfishness and greed, for the first letter in a word refers to the writer, the last to his relations with others, and here the hooks are pointing to the first letter. Since the nature of a hook is to hold on, we also see greed.

FIGURE 4.

Sorry, it will have to wait

The writer of Figure 4 has long beginning strokes, extended well under the body of the writing. He is ambitious—shown by the distance he has come—but he will grate on other peoples' nerves, for he needs a lot of room for himself and will get in their way.

FIGURE 5.

I miss my mommy

Figure 5 shows a long extension to the left of the body of the writing. It indicates one with strong ties to the past, and a need to stretch out to the left.

FIGURE 6.

Lovsy Headache

In Figure 6 the beginning strokes touch the letter—not in the usual way, but as if there were some unconscious motive in the writer. These beginning strokes touch the stems of the letters in the upper area, corresponding to the head. This writer feels a mental strain in whatever he does, as if someone were poking something at his head.

The end stroke represents a man's true personality, whereas the beginning stroke represents what he sees in himself and what he wants others to see in him. The end stroke shows the reality of how he relates to his fellowman. The beginning letter demonstrates his self-image, while the end stroke demonstrates his true feelings about the one he is writing to.

In general, a man starts off trying to give the best possible impression of himself, and this shows in the beginning stroke. After a while, he lets his guard down, and at the end he is not so conscious as he was of giving that good first impression. He has asserted himself; he no longer needs to be so conscious of his appearance. Therefore we see his true character emerge. It is always interesting to compare the beginning strokes with the end ones, a comparison that yields a wealth of information.

With the end stroke, the writer has a problem similar to that of his beginning stroke—where to end. It is a social decision, since the end of the word represents his relationship to his fellowman. If his end stroke turns back toward the left, this shows his thinking is directed toward the past, his home, mother and childhood, repression. If it is drawn out to the right, it shows him oriented toward other people, the future, goals. If his end strokes go upward, we will see that his thoughts are spiritual ones, religious, even mystical. If they go downward, his thoughts are materialistic, sexual, implying that he lives a life of pleasure. If he avoids a commitment and simply fades out, without an end stroke at all, it indicates meanness toward his fellowman. Let us examine some end strokes and make these points more vivid.

FIGURE 7.

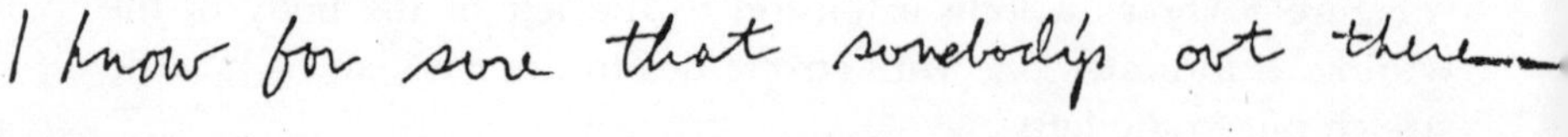

I know for sure that somebody's out there

When the last letter of the line is continued on to the edge of the page, as in Figure 7, bypassing any possible margin, the writer is trying to occupy a space he fears someone else may. This shows mistrust as well as fear. These are the people who have three and four locks on every door and are always checking up on them, as though expecting someone to intrude.

FIGURE 8.

Figure 8 shows the end stroke turning back and actually crossing the first letter of the writer's name, which represents his ego. He therefore has deleted his ego, himself. He is greatly disappointed in himself, to the point where he may commit suicide, since he is stabbing himself (his ego) through the heart.

Observe the end stroke of George Bernard Shaw's signature in Figure 8A. The end stroke of the *S* cuts sharply back through his

FIGURE 8A.

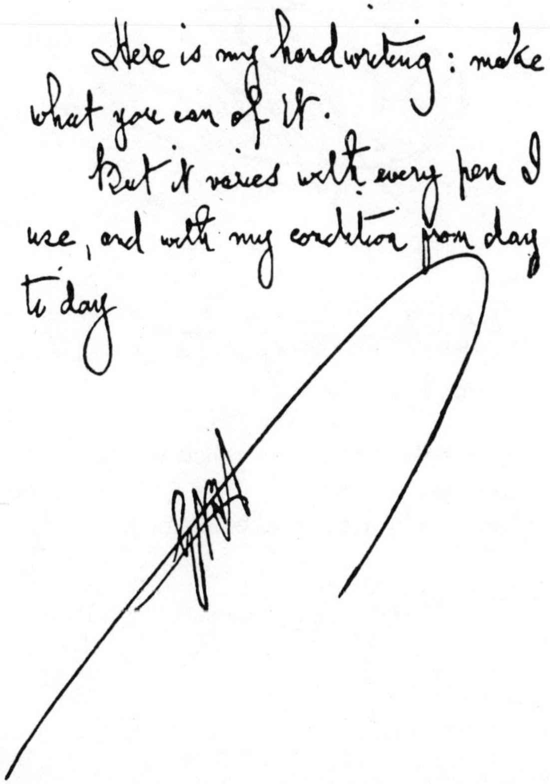

initials. This endstroke shows that in spite of his achievements, George Bernard Shaw had difficulty feeling "important."

FIGURE 9.

In Figure 9 we see the end stroke completely encircling the name. This writer wants to feel protected, so he encloses himself from all sides. In fact, he often likes to trap others in the spider web he has formed. This type of person is often paranoid as well, fearing the outside world.

Paranoia and lack of trust are traits found in the writing of the French physicist and discoverer of the "law of volumes," Joseph Louis Gay Lussac (Figure 9A):

FIGURE 9A.

FIGURE 10.

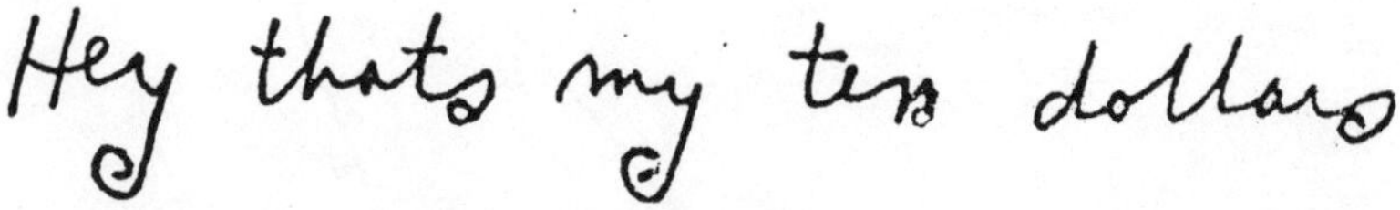

Figure 10 shows the end stroke rolled up into a shape we call a claw. Claws are used to grab, so we see greed, and the fact that the claw points back to himself shows egotism.

FIGURE 11.

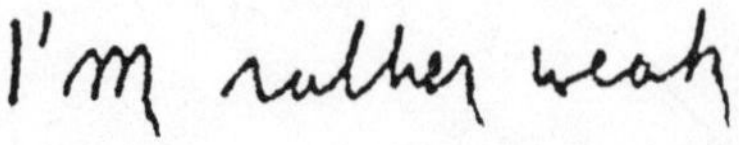

When the stroke extends downward in a much weaker fashion than the rest of the word, as in Figure 11, we see fatigue, weakness, possibly ill-health. This droopy writing reflects the writer's lack of physical well-being.

FIGURE 12.

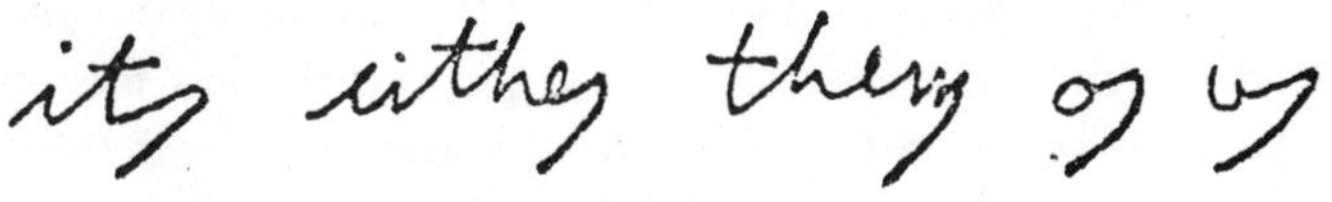

Figure 12 shows the end stroke descending toward the left, in the form of an arcade. An arcade is one of the various forms of connections between letters and generally shows that the writer would prefer to be impenetrable. (Forms of connections will be discussed in a later chapter.)

Besides being on the defensive, this person would prefer to keep away from others. The descending end stroke can be viewed as a stick of some kind, while the writer (represented by the word which this stroke finishes off) stands safely behind it—thereby keeping the other person at a distance.

FIGURE 13.

The end stroke of Figure 13 covers the whole word. This shows an urge to protect, as if the writer were putting a roof over his home. Notice that the stroke is in the upper zone; this urge to protect was perhaps brought on by spiritual feelings.

FIGURE 14.

Figure 14 shows the end strokes thickening. And since the end strokes reflect the writer's relationship with other human beings, we can interpret this thickened approach as a club he holds over their heads. This indicates brutality.

If the end stroke were merely turned up, without thickening, it would indicate bravery. It is as though he raised his hands in an urge to go beyond the call of duty.

An end stroke that points down, particularly if heavy and pointed, indicates cold-heartedness.

FIGURE 15.

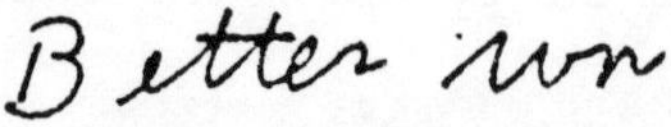

Better run

Figure 15 shows the last downstroke of the last letter not reaching the bottom of the base line. Picture a man with one foot on the ground and the other in the air, running somewhere. If this writer witnesses an accident or is placed in a position where he could offer needed help, he will not come forward. He prefers to run away and not become involved; he won't admit things and doesn't want others to know who he really is. If he should be pinned down, he will find a way of concealing what he knows.

FIGURE 16.

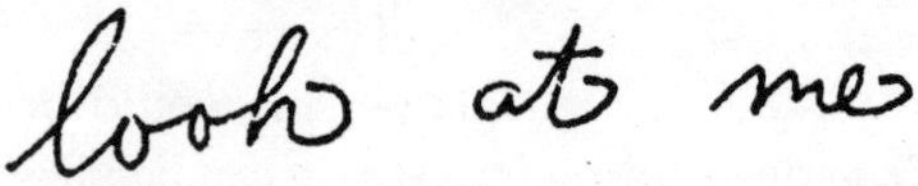

look at me

In Figure 16 the end stroke turns back to the left in a pointing fashion. The writer is trying to bring attention to himself. It shows egotism. Note: This is a straight line after the turn, not a claw.

FIGURE 17.

never!

Figure 17 shows no end stroke. Since the end stroke represents the writer's relationship to his fellowman, this person obviously doesn't give a drop of himself to others. He has done his "duty" by barely completing the word (any less and the letter would not have been recognizable as an *r*). This shows meanness, one who does not relate well to others.

When this downstroke is extended, it indicates a kind of *stressed indifference*—or even cruelty.

FIGURE 18.

Hi, How are you

Figure 18 shows simple writing with a moderate degree of extension of the end stroke. This shows a good, normal relationship with others.

FIGURE 19.

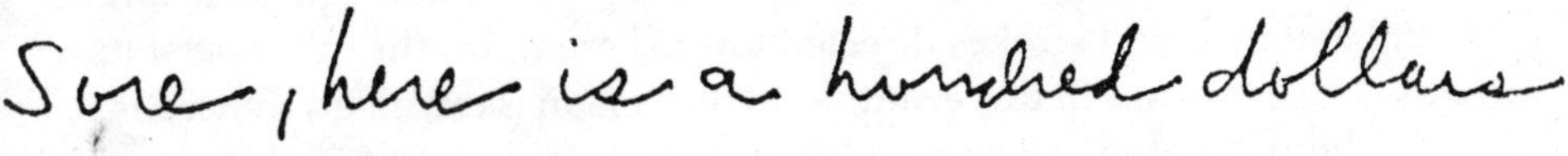

Sure, here is a hundred dollars

Figure 19 shows the end strokes considerably extended, and in this we recognize a generous, giving nature on the part of the writer.

Notice the end strokes of Joan Crawford's script in Figure 19A, especially in "you" (top line) showing generosity by its extension to the right.

FIGURE 19A.

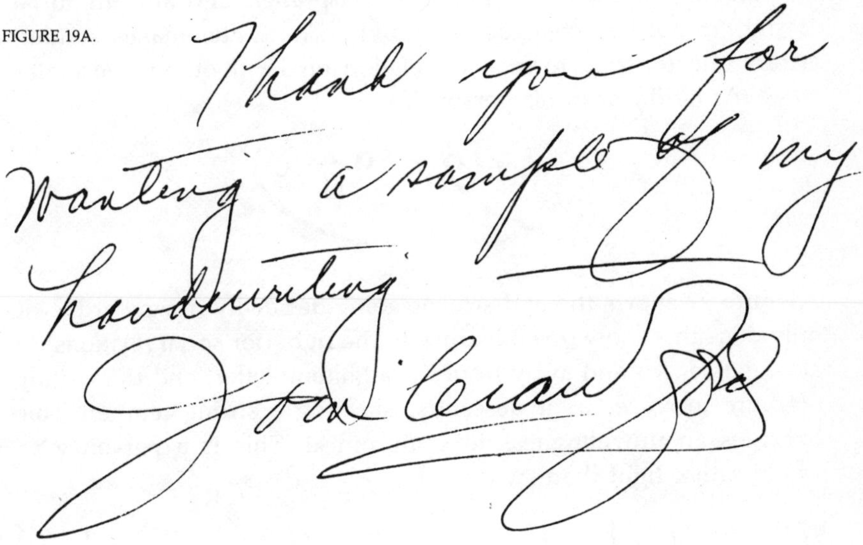

Thank you for wanting a sample of my handwriting

Joan Crawford

FIGURE 20.

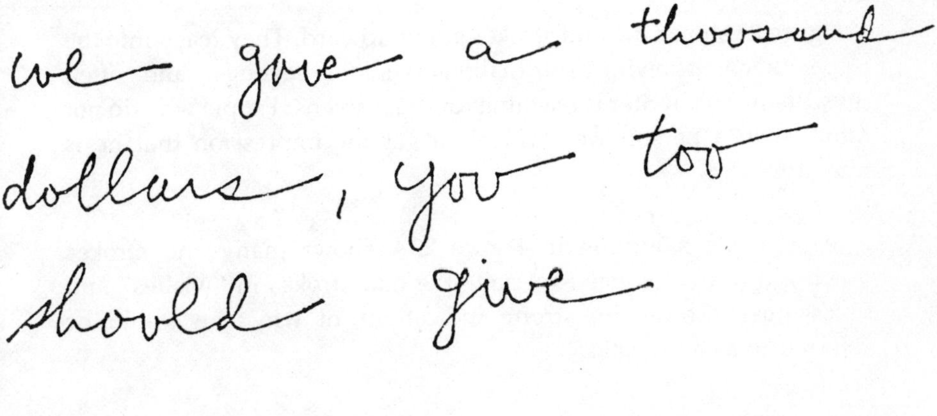

we gave a thousand dollars, you too should give

Figure 20 shows extremely long end strokes. (Note: Figures 18 and 19 have their end strokes directed toward the right, the other person, as is also the case in this example.) This person is extremely generous, but he will get on other people's nerves because his attitude toward them is intolerant: If he gave, they must too.

FIGURE 21.

Better cancel our date

Figure 21 shows the end strokes extended, showing good social relationships; however, it ends in a sharp angle and appears to be saying, "Stop! I've changed my mind." The writer makes sudden last-minute decisions to break off relationships with others; the angles show the hardness in his personality.

FIGURE 22.

never again

Figure 22 shows the end strokes going decidedly downward. Not only does this show no end stroke to the right (for social relations), it also goes down and away from the adjoining letter, and the writing pressure increases as it descends, showing a strong temper. This indicates an unwillingness to compromise. This is a person who would rather fight than switch.

FIGURE 23.

I'm a spiritual person

Figure 23 shows the end strokes going upward. They reach into the upper zone, showing spirituality, religious feelings, and often mysticism. This writer is reaching for the heavens. People who do not know such a person well will often get the impression that he is immature.

Jeane Dixon's writing in Figure 23A shows many end strokes veering upward. Notice especially the end strokes in "wishes" and "blessings." These are strong indications of why she would be referred to as a "mystic."

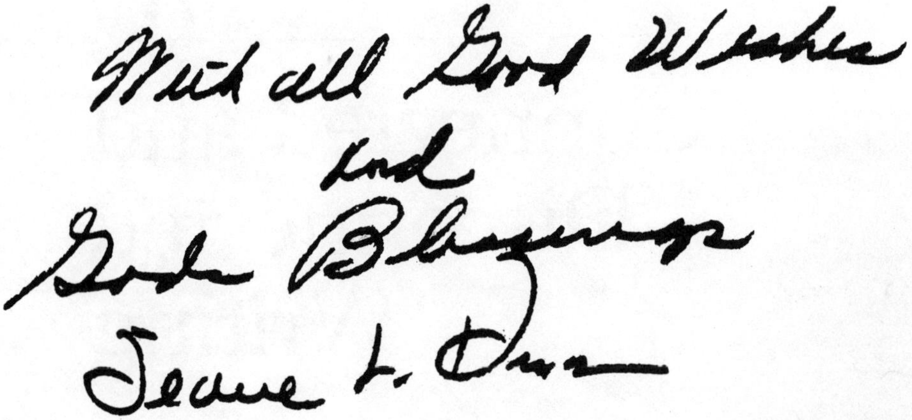

FIGURE 23A.

Figure 24 shows the end strokes going over and down to the left side of the last letter. It would appear that this writer allows information to go in one ear and out the other. He distorts facts and feels that he is deceiving others.

FIGURE 24.

10

Connected and Disconnected Writing

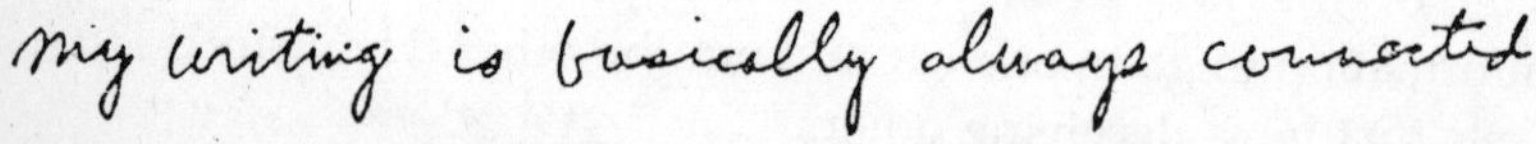

my writing is basically always connected

Figure 1 shows an example of *connected writing*. One of the major points that the graphologist looks for in his analysis is how the subject thinks. In this example, we see that each word is internally connected, each letter linked to the following one. Connected writing shows a person who is both practical and logical. He will take his time figuring something out, but once he has done so, he is very tenacious of his opinion. He is the person who builds fact upon fact, then adds them up to a logical decision. Graphologists consider this masculine writing.

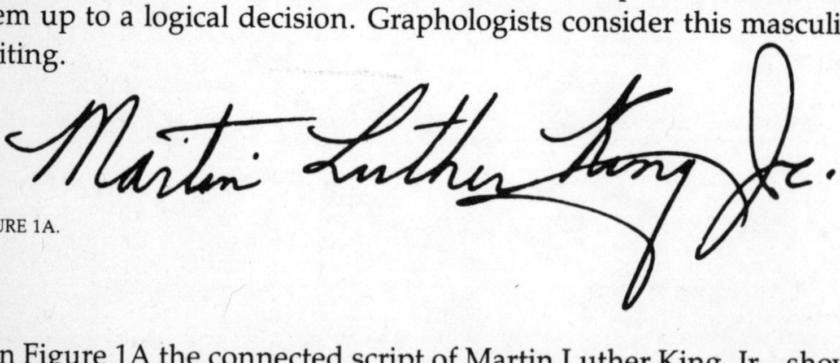

Martin Luther King Jr.

FIGURE 1A.

In Figure 1A the connected script of Martin Luther King, Jr., shows both logic and pragmatism.

FIGURE 2.

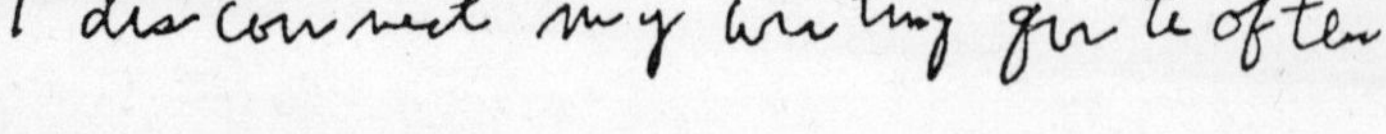

I disconnect my writing quite often

Figure 2 shows *disconnected writing*—disconnected most of the time. There's a touch of femininity in disconnected writings. Its nature is intuitive. Since most of this person's writing is disconnected, his emphasis is on his intuition. He is also capable of logic (he does connect some of his letters), and when he needs the logical thought processes, he is able to draw them forth. Disconnection also implies imagination, so this writer is excellent to have around when an idea is needed. Because of his hunches—which are often right—he is a quicker thinker than the connected writer, and he has usually sized up the situation and come to a decision while the connected writer is still putting facts together.

This writer sometimes comes to grief over his hunches, however. Because they are so often correct, he is inclined to think they always are. On some occasion he may demand that his position be respected, refusing to admit that he drew it from intuition and not fact, and will hang on stubbornly to his opinion beyond all logical objections.

Notice the handwriting of French philosopher and Nobel Prize winner Henri Bergson (Figure 2A). He has an extreme degree of disconnection in his writing, along with precisely placed *i* dots—a powerful intuition allied with alertness to details and a precise memory. Thus he was able to analyze the function of intuition in the thinking process:

FIGURE 2A.

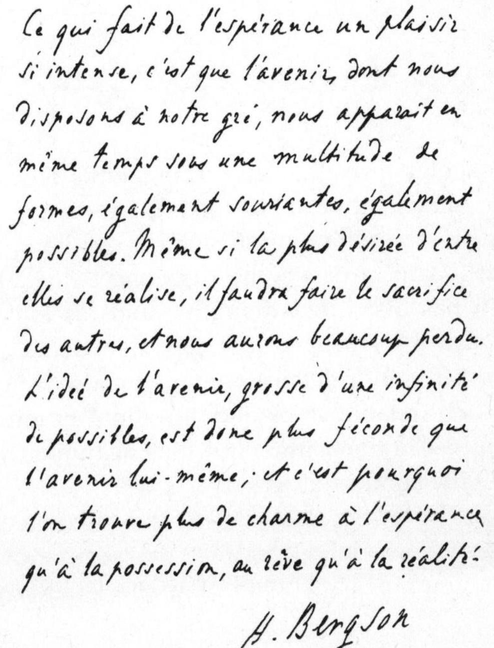
Ce qui fait de l'espérance un plaisir
si intense, c'est que l'avenir, dont nous
disposons à notre gré, nous apparaît en
même temps sous une multitude de
formes, également souriantes, également
possibles. Même si la plus désirée d'entre
elles se réalise, il faudra faire le sacrifice
des autres, et nous aurons beaucoup perdu.
L'idée de l'avenir, grosse d'une infinité
de possibles, est donc plus féconde que
l'avenir lui-même; et c'est pourquoi
l'on trouve plus de charme à l'espérance
qu'à la possession, au rêve qu'à la réalité.

H. Bergson

Two outstanding personality traits hit the eye immediately in the signature of the Italian painter Leonardo da Vinci—the pressure and the high degree of disconnection. Pressure often indicates sensuality and love of color, and disconnectedness shows a high degree of intuition.

FIGURE 2B.

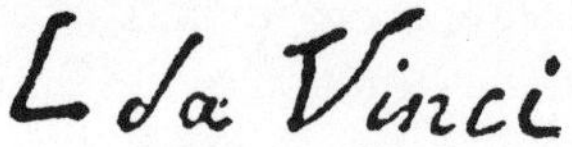

FIGURE 2C.

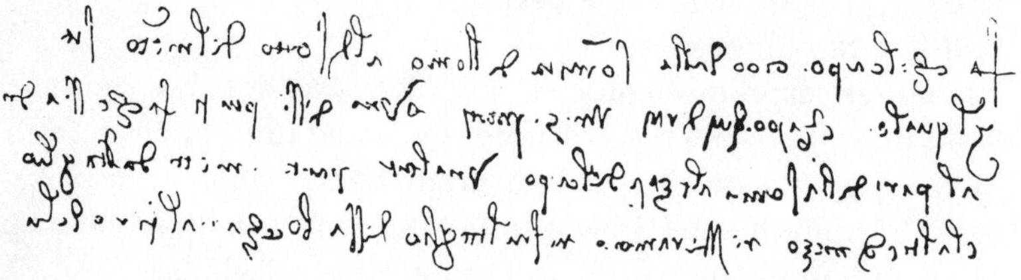

Figure 2C shows a fine example of "mirror writing" by Leonardo Da Vinci. This kind of writing, often written by left-handed writers (Leonardo was ambidextrous, though favoring his left hand) can easily be read by holding it up to a mirror. In such a strongly disconnected script such as this, much femininity is indicated.

FIGURE 3.

Figure 3 shows disconnected writing—this time, completely disconnected. Almost none of the letters are connected, whereas in Figure 2 some are. This writer tends to be impractical, moody, a daydreamer. Many artists write disconnectedly. The disconnected writer often has disjointed thoughts, and his logical thought processes are also disconnected. He can be extremely bright and will show interest in minor details when given a set of facts. He is quite distant in social relationships and is seldom in touch with his own feelings. Because of the manner in which he thinks, he is often looked down on by the connected writer.

A person who prints is similar to the disconnected writer. This writing often shows immaturity. If the sample of handwriting is printed, the graphologist should request a letter written in script in addition, for only a limited number of facts can be gathered from printed writing.

FIGURE 4.

A. *Connection*

B. *Connection*

C. disconnection

Many writings *look* totally disconnected, but actually are not—those where one letter ends and the next letter begins very close together and in direct line, as in Figure 4B. If the writer had connected the writing, the connection would have followed the same route and simply inked in the blank space. It is almost as though a connected piece of writing had been carefully cut into individual letters.

Graphologically speaking, Figure 4B has the effect of being connected. There is strong intuition here, which the writer prefers to the connected, logical approach. This writer does have relationships, and his thoughts have a definite logical link.

Figure 4C shows total disconnection. There is no connection between where one letter ends and the next begins. This writer, totally intuitive, usually relies on his hunches and has great difficulty backing up his decisions logically.

FIGURE 5.

Beside letters I also connect my words

Figure 5 shows writing that not only connects the letters, but the words themselves. Stubborn is the word to describe this person. When he gets an idea, he sticks by it, right or wrong. He has many principles. When he enters a heated discussion, he refuses to give way until long after he has alienated the other participants.

It should be borne in mind that connections always represent building fact upon fact. Any break will let intuition seep in. It is said that in many professions, including that of writing, where a person does not want his logical train of thought derailed by intuition, he will find himself connecting words together, leaving not even minute spaces to upset his thinking pattern. Notice the many connections between words and in the signatures of W. Somerset Maugham (Figure 5A) and Sir Walter Scott (Figure 5B):

FIGURE 5A.

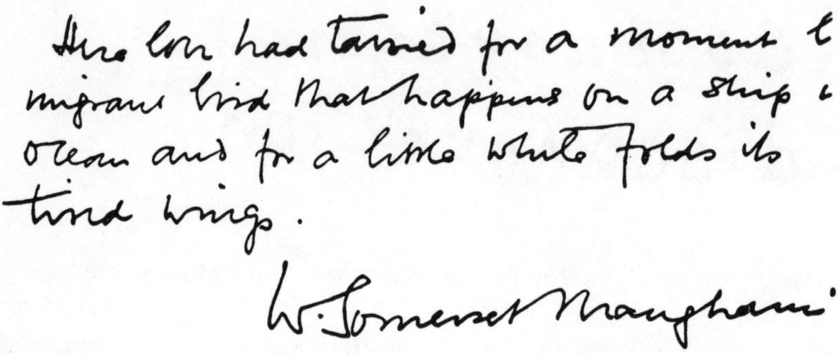

FIGURE 5B.

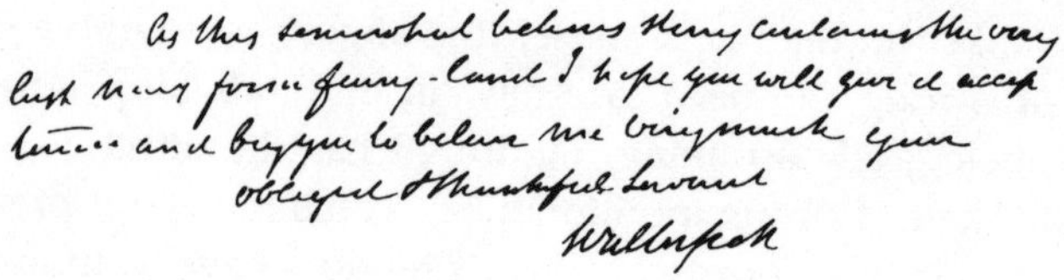

11
Forms of
Connection

When the expression *form of connection* is used, it means how the upstrokes and the downstrokes are connected—usually somewhere in the middle zone. Should the connections occur in another zone, particular emphasis is being shown by the writer in all that this particular zone represents. Since the connecting strokes by nature meet in the middle zone and the middle zone is indicative of the writer's social relationships, it gives the graphologist strong insight into the writer's social life.

There are four major types of connections: *arcade, garland, angular,* and *thready*. Often the graphologist finds more than one form of connection in the same writing. If one form is used more frequently than the others, the writer probably has the qualities reflected by that particular form of connection. However, although one form may be the dominant one in the writer's personality, the characteristics of the other forms do exist and play a role in his personality also. When we have two connecting forms (or even more, though it is not frequent) used approximately equally, we say that the writer possesses the personality traits of the two forms in equal proportion.

The Arcade Connection:

FIGURE 1.

Figure 1 shows reserve in the personality, someone who would rather be with nature than with people. Arcade writers are often secretive, have a strong interest in architecture (the arcade itself resembles an arch), and are frequently artists. The arcade writer prefers to shut the world out and often puts on a facade. With the arcade connection to protect him, he can make believe that he is someone he really isn't.

The arcade writer is usually slower in his reactions than most people, especially those who write in garland connections (see Figure 2). In writing the arcade, the subject must use an up-down direction, employing extensor muscles—muscles used in extending a limb. The garland writer, on the other hand, uses down-up direction, employing flexor muscles—muscles used in bending or clenching a limb. The flexors are stronger than the extensors, and hence it is easier and quicker to write the garland than the arcade.

The Garland Connection:

FIGURE 2.

The major personality trait of the garland writer, as in Figure 2, is a love of peace. Garland writers are fond of pleasure, will always try to find the easy way out, and try to avoid conflicts. They usually have a great deal of charm. Their receptive personalities and willingness to be exposed to whatever may come can be seen by the openness at the top of their letters. They are warm, loving, patient persons and are often found in positions where it is necessary to deal directly with people. They get along well with others and know how to use their charm when it is needed. Observe the handwriting of Dr. David Livingstone in Figure 2A:

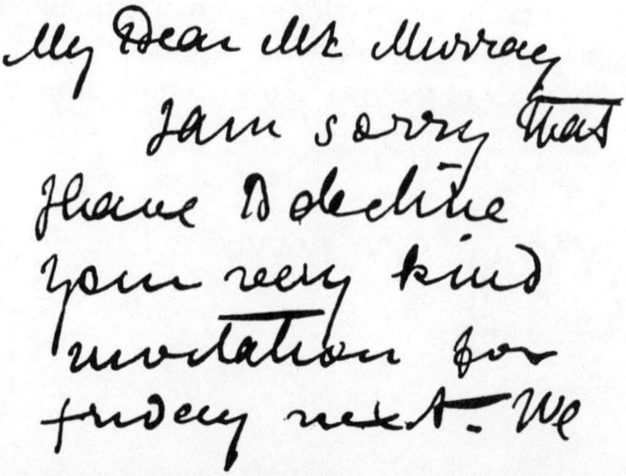

FIGURE 2A.

The many garlands in Dr. Livingstone's writing show a closeness to nature, perhaps a positive aspect in working in the jungle, and the angles show a rigidity necessary for the job.

The Angular Connection:

FIGURE 3.

The writer of the angular connection, as in Figure 3, has a lively, vibrant personality and is alert and competitive. He has a critical mind, and when he starts a job, he finishes it. He is hard and aggressive and can be difficult to get along with—as shown by the angles, which indicate rigidity. He is quick, both physically and mentally. He will often clash with the person writing the arcade form of connection, since the arcade writer tends to be slower coming to decisions. The writer of the angular connection often loses patience with the arcade writer for his procrastination. The arcade writer, in turn, feels persecuted and badgered for acting in ways that are natural to him.

FIGURE 3A.

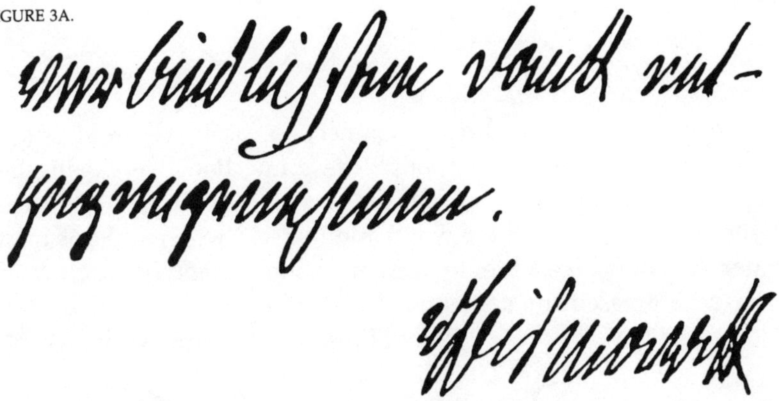

Observe the angular, rigid handwritings of Otto Von Bismarck (Figure 3A) and Robert F. Kennedy (Figure 3B). Bismarck's writing is angular both on top (mental rigidity) and on bottom (emotional toughness); Robert F. Kennedy's is angular on top, showing his

FIGURE 3B.

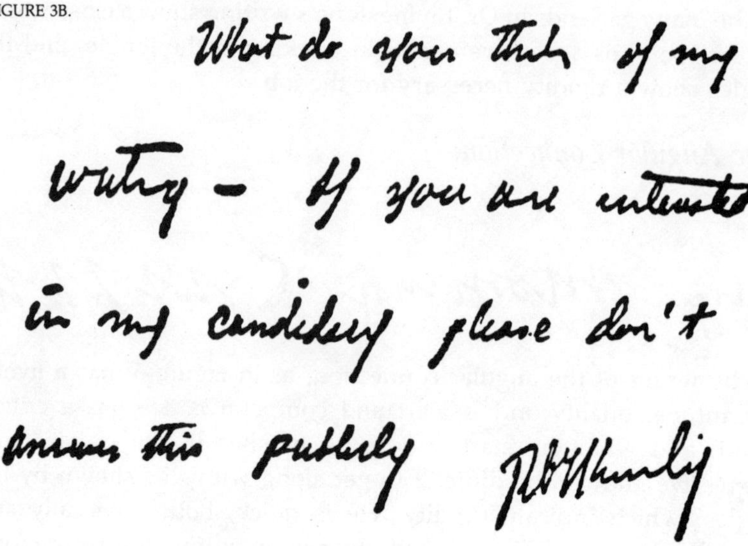

What do you think of my

writing — If you are interested

in my candidacy please don't

answer this publicly

mental keenness, but rounded at the bottom, showing a pliability of emotions.

The Thready Connection:

FIGURE 4.

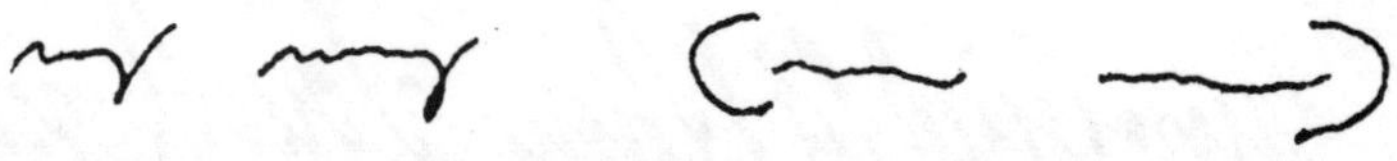

The example of the thready connection, as in Figure 4, should speak for itself. It looks as though the connections were being held together by pieces of thread. This is very quick writing. The thready writer is unsure of both the world and himself, with emphasis on the latter. It is difficult for him to make up his mind, and he would prefer not to be pressed for decisions. This writing often shows hysteria. Notice the handwriting of former President Richard Nixon:

FIGURE 4A.

FIGURE 4B.

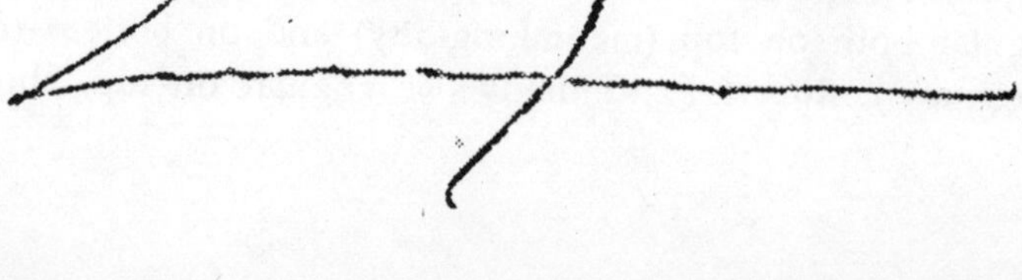

Figure 4A was written in 1959, when Nixon was Vice-President of the United States. It is written with strength and clarity. Figure 4B was written during the Watergate affair, a most sensitive period. This form should not be mistaken for the threadlike dying out of words shown in Figure 5.

FIGURE 5.

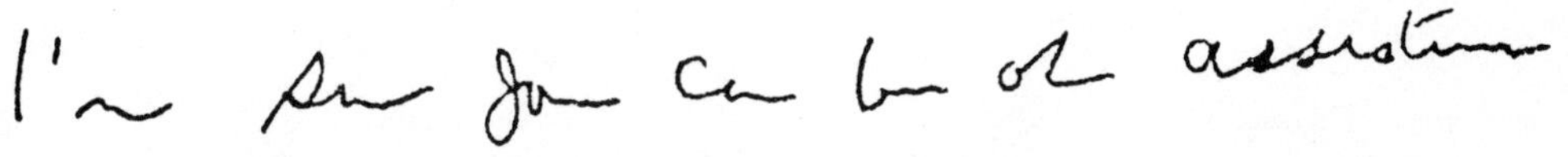

Here the middle zone starts at a certain height and dwindles to about the size of a thread as it ends. This shows powerful intuition, always wiggling out of difficult situations (notice how the form resembles that of a snake). This writer definitely prefers not to commit himself to any definite course of action. Many diplomats write in this threadlike form.

12

Pressure

One of the most important ways of finding out whether a person is extroverted, introverted, or ambiverted is by looking at his writing pressure. Pressure is a sign of how forceful the individual is.

But first we have to make sure that the writing tool is the one the writer usually employs. The amount of pressure one uses reflects the libido—the strength of the individual. So if the subject were to use a much heavier writing tool than he ordinarily does (or vice versa), the result would obviously not reflect his true writing strength. Many graphologists say that the more physically minded the individual is and the more drive he has, the more apt he is to use a heavier writing tool than his counterpart. This heavier writing tool suits his personality. The more spiritually motivated writer, with less physical drive, would be more likely to use a lighter writing tool.

Still, it is important for the graphologist to be aware of variations. In any given day, a healthy individual can go through quite a few changes of mood, so if the writer is naturally an "up" person and an analysis were done of him at a time in the day when he was "down," then this analysis would probably be an inaccurate reflection of his permanent personality traits. Thus, when we do an analysis, we like to have as much written material as possible taken from different periods.

FIGURE 1.

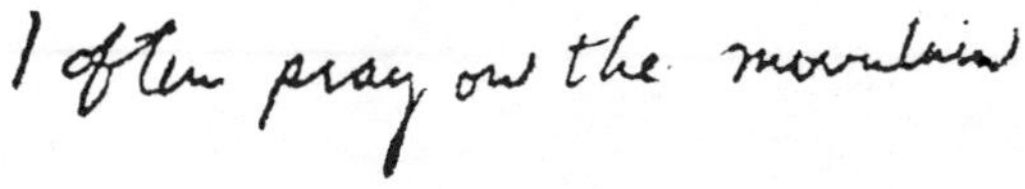

In Figure 1 we see light pressure. The writing is quite fine, almost threadlike. This writer's major personality trait is his sensitivity. He is usually idealistic, often spiritual, and is affected by what goes on around him. In contrast to these "soft" traits, he often seems to be quite critical. He is an introvert, and yet many people who write with light pressure go against their basic natures to take on outgoing, high-pressure jobs—that of salesman, for example.

FIGURE 2.

Figure 2 shows heavy pressure. This writer's major drives are physical (try writing this hand and see how much strength it requires). He is materialistic, forceful, rarely modest. At work, if perseverance is necessary, he is the man for the job, for he rarely gives up. He has natural energy and is determined to succeed. He enjoys being among people, is an extrovert, and prefers a "fast" crowd. Notice the handwriting of Chairman Mao Tse-tung in Figure 2B and that of Fidel Castro in Figure 2A. One thing the two men have in common is the pressure they exert while writing—a strong indication of forceful personality. It makes no difference that Chairman Mao's writing is in his native Chinese, for the strength of the personality shows through, whatever the language.

FIGURE 2A.

FIGURE 2B.

FIGURE 3.

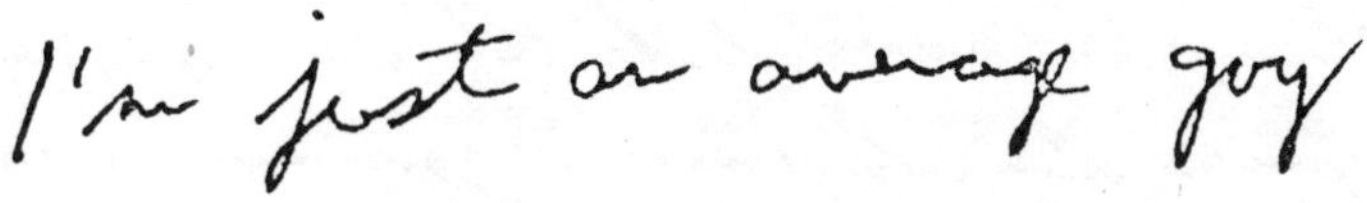

I'm just an average guy

Most people write as in Figure 3, with medium pressure. This writer is the happy balance between the previous two, neither overly sensitive nor overly materialistic. Because he does not have these excesses, it is much easier for him to be understood than the other two—he is an ambivert.

These points about pressure can be further broken down. When we have light pressure with small middle-zone letters, we see a writer who is inventive (remember that small middle-zone letters indicate the scientific thinker) as well as sensitive. Light pressure with larger and rounder middle-zone letters reveals sensitivity manifesting itself in helping others and cooperating with them.

When the light-pressured writing has an irregular base line and the *t* bar is both small and light, we see the born follower. The light pressure shows him to be sensitive, not the aggressive type. When he writes the irregular base line, his thinking is not straight, and small and light *t* bars show him to have a lack of confidence.

The light-pressured writer can have an occasional heavier stroke. In that case, though he may be sensitive, he probably is prone to sudden outbursts of temper and lacks patience, expressed by the sudden appearance of the heavy strokes.

A heavy-pressured writing that shows uniqueness, especially in the capitals (representing the ego), will indicate qualities of leadership. Such a writer thinks big. The heavy pressure indicates strength of personality, and his sense of his own uniqueness shows up in his capitals. These qualities combined make him a true leader.

FIGURE 4.

Hey, get out of my way!

Figure 4 shows heavy-pressured writing coupled with muddy writing. This writer is extremely sensuous, difficult to control, and often violent. The accent is on the physical. Notice the writing of former "Mr. America" Alan Stephen in Figure 4A:

FIGURE 4A.

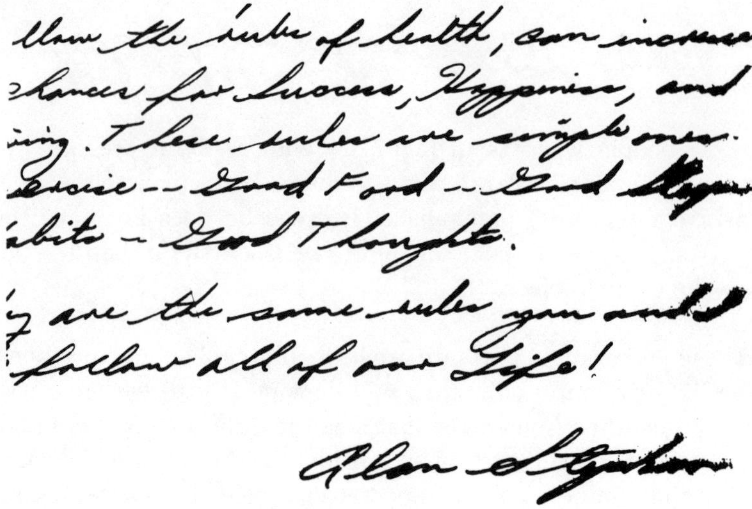

Pressure that constantly varies, from light to medium to heavy or any other order, indicates a person who is in the process of changing. This does not necessarily mean a youngster, for many older people go through changes in life-style, too. This illustrates why the graphologist cannot determine the chronological age of the writer.

Inconsistent pressure can also be an indication of emotional imbalance. Notice the blatant inconsistency of pressure in the handwriting of the assasin of President McKinley, Leon Czolgosz, in Figure 4B:

FIGURE 4B.

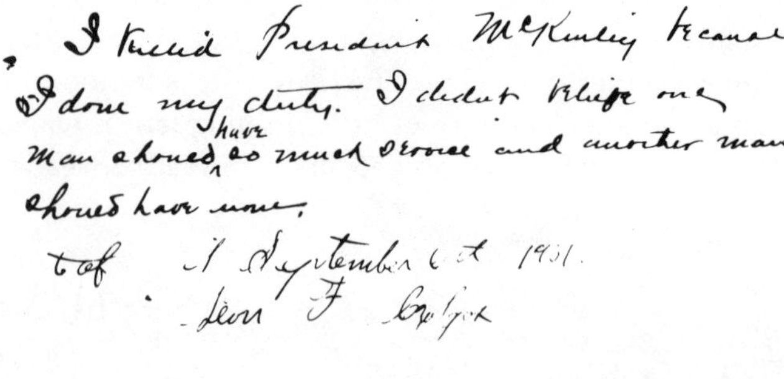

Thus all the conflicting aspects of the personality are represented by the various types of pressures, and the graphologist therefore requires various samples of writing from different periods of time to make a complete analysis.

13

Loops

In a general sense, loops shows us the mental attitude of the writer.

FIGURE 1.

Figure 1 shows neither an upper loop nor a lower one, only single strokes. If there had been loops, they would not have made the letters more readable. This writer reduces everything to its simplest form. Any stroke that is not essential is omitted. As long as the word is readable, why add loops? In whatever this writer does, his method is direct.

FIGURE 1A.

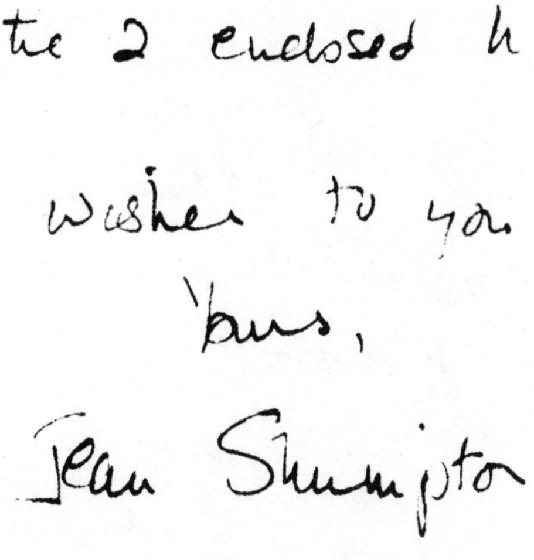

81

Directness and intelligence are indicated in Jean Shrimpton's handwriting (Figure 1A). Notice the simplified strokes: the *h* in "wishes" and in her surname; the *d* in "enclosed"; the downstrokes in "you" and "yours." This is quite an uncluttered hand.

FIGURE 2.

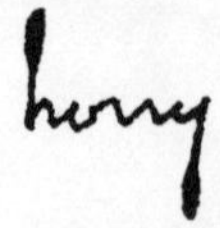

Figure 2 shows the same characteristics as Figure 1. There are no loops, but the top and bottom strokes are written thickly and bluntly, so we find, in addition to directness, that the writer is opinionated and impatient to finish the job (the heavy pressure accentuates what the strokes themselves have already shown, directness and speed).

FIGURE 2A.

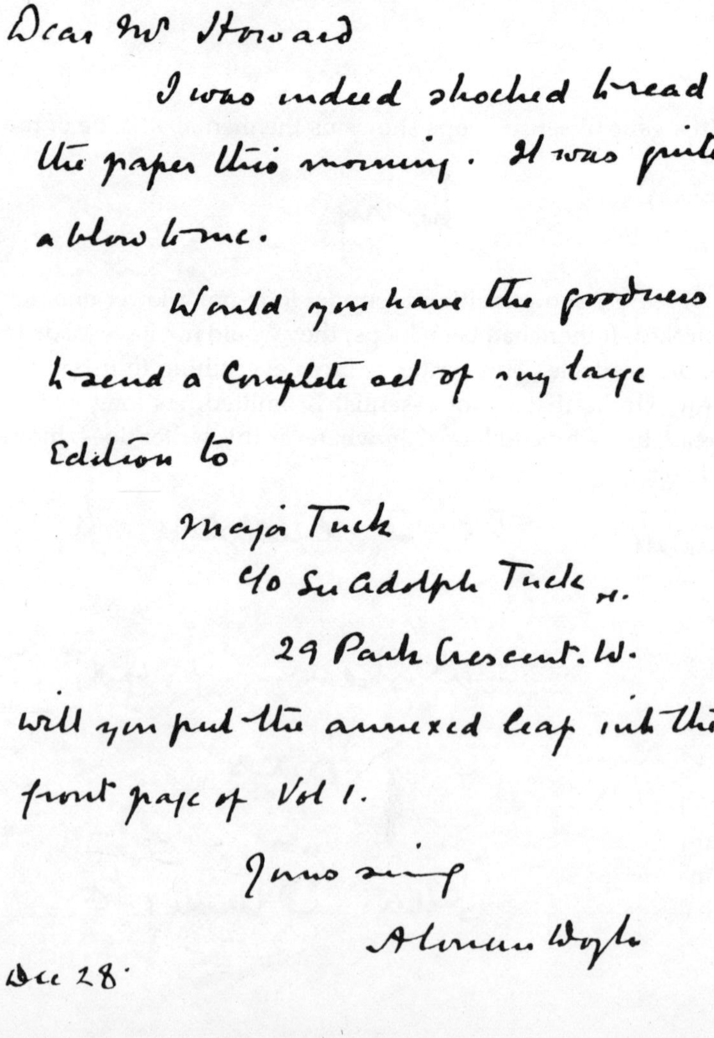

Dear Mr Howard

I was indeed shocked to read the paper this morning. It was quite a blow to me.

Would you have the goodness to send a Complete set of my large Edition to

Major Tuck
C/o Sir Adolph Tuck
29 Park Crescent. W.

Will you put the annexed leaf into the front page of Vol 1.

Yours sincerely
Arthur Conan Doyle

Dec 28.

Figure 2A shows the handwriting of Arthur Conan Doyle. To be a top-notch investigator one must break things down to their essentials, gleaning the important out of the unimportant. Observe the key word "lean" in Arthur Conan Doyle's writing. The upper- and underlengths are both unlooped and thick, showing directness. Anything that is not essential (loops) is not there to clutter his mind, hence, the investigator. Sherlock Holmes's author also reveals impatience by having these strokes thick (blunt).

Notice the similarity in the writing of Dr. Karl A. Menninger in Figure 2B:

FIGURE 2B

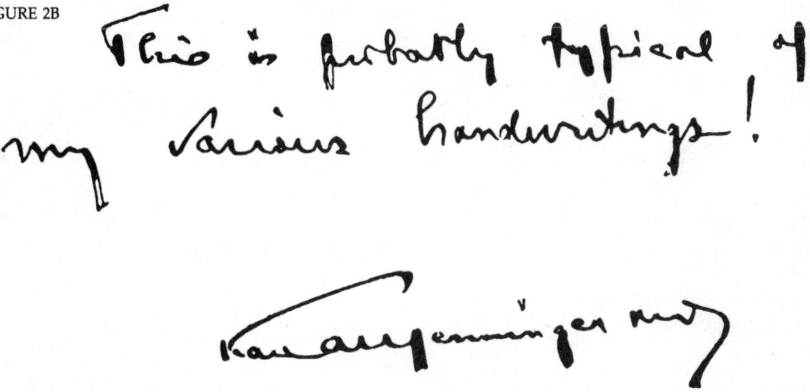

Figure 3 shows tall, thin loops. Thinness of the loop in the upper (intellectual) area shows cautious thinking, skepticism. The height of the loop shows spiritual meaning and a lack of materialism.

FIGURE 3.

FIGURE 4.

Figure 4 shows the upper loops both high and wide. Like Figure 3, this example also shows aspirations, but the accent is on the materialistic aspect of aspiration. Think of this upper loop as a balloon. The writer is flying. He wants very much to be noticed.

FIGURE 5.

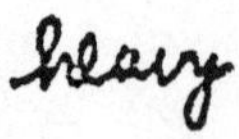

heavy

Figure 5 shows a relatively short upper loop. This writer is cautious in his thinking. He is not willing to indulge himself in flights of spirituality. When the rest of his writing shows unusual traits (unique techniques, forms not often found) we see a person with strong concentration and critical ability. The more ornamented and full of flourishes the writing, the less power of concentration the writer has. Here we see little to obstruct the writer's concentration.

14

The Letters

Each sign in an analysis has meaning, but is reliable only as one aspect of the total analysis. So although the following letters are strong indicators by themselves, they cannot be regarded as proof of any fact about the writer until they are properly weighed.

There are many different ways of forming the letters of the alphabet:

A

FIGURE 1.

Figure 1 shows two hooks. A hook by nature grabs, hence it shows greed. The double hook implies avarice.

FIGURE 2.

The left leg in Figure 2 is extended far to the left (past). The fact that there is also a blotch hints of a "blotch" in the writer's past, which is very much on his mind.

A

FIGURE 3.

The letter in Figure 3 is called a block letter. Its construction is simplified, showing intelligence and culture. Most books use block letters, and this may be an unconscious imitation.

FIGURE 4.

The markings on top of the letter in Figure 4 are inexact and unnecessary. This shows inexactness on the part of the writer, but the fact that he did write the letter in such a manner shows him to be an unusual character.

FIGURE 5.

The letter in Figure 5 shows a large loop with a knot. Loops made bigger than necessary to read the letter show pride. This particular form has been found among writers who take pride in their families.

FIGURE 6.

In Figure 6 we see a knot, which shows toughness, hardness—someone who is apt to be thorough in what he undertakes and will not give up easily.

FIGURE 7.

The letter in Figure 7 should not be confused with that in Figure 2. Here the starting point of the letter is close to the body, not extended to the left. The thick writing shows a materialistic nature.

FIGURE 8.

Capital letters, among other things, show an image of ego. Thus the thin, narrow capital letter in Figure 8 indicates shyness.

FIGURE 9.

In Figure 9 the left leg is considerably longer than the right one, as if the man were running. It shows aggression and ambition.

FIGURE 10.

Figure 10 is a round block letter. It depicts a form of construction of some kind and therefore shows a constructive thinker.

FIGURE 11.

The letter in Figure 11 is similar to that in Figure 10. It is constructed in a square fashion, showing an interest in architecture or in mechanically related fields. The shape itself looks like a building brick.

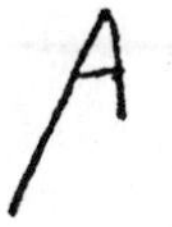

FIGURE 12.

In Figure 12 the left leg is considerably longer than the right, like that in Figure 9, but it descends much deeper. We see in this the meddler. Because of the position he gets himself into, the writer will become argumentative when the person he is annoying flares up at him.

FIGURE 13.

In Figure 13 we see a capital *A* in the form of a small *a*. Since the capital letter shows the ego of the writer, a small letter indicates humility and modesty.

FIGURE 14.

In Figure 14 the bar of the *A* is missing. It shows carelessness and neglect. There are times when the *A* bar may be omitted and not have these meanings— when the writer is in a hurry, for instance—but if the writer always forms his *A*'s like this, it implies slovenliness.

FIGURE 15.

The arc in Figure 15 points back to the capital letter (the ego) and therefore shows egotism.

FIGURE 16.

In Figure 16, the left leg stretches out to the left, showing a strong attachment to the past. Often these writers have a difficult time getting started on projects or even everyday things.

FIGURE 17.

FIGURE 18.

Figures 17 and 18 show a similar characteristic to that of Figure 4, in that the crossings are inexact. Here their lack of completion forms what graphologists call open-mouthed ovals, which shows talkativeness. The more open the ovals are, the more talkative the writer is. When these letters are a regular feature of someone's writing, he can be said to be both open and honest. However, if there are only a few oval letters, it would be best not to tell the writer any secrets—he may have difficulty keeping them.

FIGURE 19.

The letter in Figure 19 shows an angular form, indicating rigidity and hardness.

Δ

FIGURE 20.

The *A* bar in Figure 20 is quite low. Like the low *t* bar, it shows an inferiority complex. Since the capital letter reflects the ego, this low bar hints at a reduced self-esteem.

FIGURE 21.

Figure 21 shows a peculiar shape. Whenever strange-looking shapes appear, we see sexual perversion and a strong sexual imagination. (However, these letters should be compared with the rest of the writing.) If this distortion is what the writer thinks the letter should look like, imagine what he thinks a sexual relationship should be.

FIGURE 22.

Though the letter in Figure 22 resembles an *A* bar, in reality it is an in-turned arc, piercing the capital (the ego). The writer is destroying his ego, showing strong depression and suicidal tendencies.

FIGURE 23.

A similar meaning is indicated when the *A* bar strongly descends as in Figure 23—its very direction implies that the writer is down in the dumps.

FIGURE 24.

The letter in Figure 24 is encircled several times, reflecting the feeling of living in one's own world of imagination. The writer is trying to protect himself by not allowing anyone else in. If anyone ever does penetrate, he will not find it easy to change the writer's ideas.

FIGURE 25.

Loops by nature are showy. Therefore in Figure 25 we see vanity. (Note: Do not confuse loops with knots, which show a different meaning).

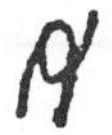

FIGURE 26.

The upward rounded stroke in Figure 26 reveals the performer, the entertainer. You can almost see him bowing to the audience as he makes this flamboyant upward stroke.

FIGURE 27.

The letter in Figure 27 is ink-filled, pasty, blotchy. It shows sensuality, as if the writer's guts were pouring out on the page from the passion inside him.

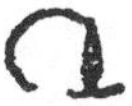

FIGURE 28.

In Figure 28, we have the oval letter open at the bottom. (Before you can analyze this letter, you must make certain that it was not the writing tool that erred. Pens do sometimes "gap.") This shows the embezzler, the crook, the hypocrite. The fact that there is something missing in its construction implies a similar lack in the

FIGURE 28A.

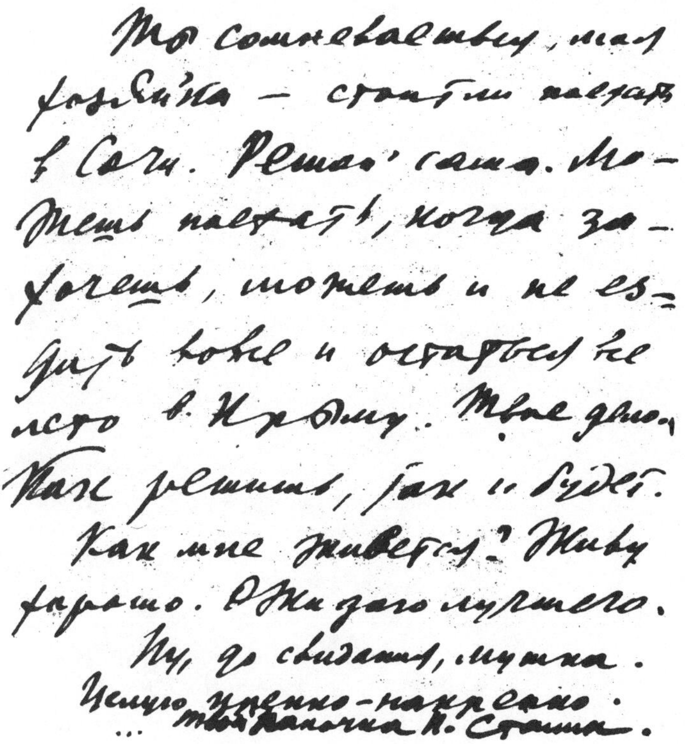

Ты сомневаешься, моя хозяйка — стоит ли поехать в Сочи. Решай сама. Можешь поехать, когда захочешь, можешь и не ездить вовсе и остаться [illegible]. Твое дело. Как решишь, так и будет.
Как мне живется? Живу хорошо. Ожидаю лучшего.
Ну, до свидания, [illegible].
Целую крепко-накрепко.
... твой папочка И. Сталин.

writer's makeup. What is missing is honesty, as though there were a hole inside him, where everything decent fell through.

Notice the handwriting of Joseph Stalin in Figure 28A, from a letter to his daughter Svetlana: The first word in the second line from the top has the *a* open at the bottom. So does the first word in the fourth line from the bottom. There may be more than we can detect, for the muddy, pastose writing, indicating brutality, may cover them up.

a

FIGURE 29.

The letter in Figure 29 shows the left side of the oval open. This writer cleverly conceals this side of his nature (the opening is tiny), but his motive is strictly for himself, and he is greedy. Obviously he is also untrustworthy. Often people who write like this are found to be neurotic.

R

FIGURE 30.

The person who writes as in Figure 30, as if he were bending away from something that may hurt him, reveals himself as touchy and sensitive. The inward-bent right stroke shows him protecting himself.

a

FIGURE 31.

The letter in Figure 31 is knotted (not to be confused with Figure 25, which is looped). The knot shows that, although the letter was already closed, the writer added the knot, just to make sure. It shows secretiveness, a reserved manner, introversion, one who rarely allows people to get to know him. When coupled with other signs in the writing, this form often appears in the writing of dishonest people.

a

FIGURE 32.

The letter in Figure 32 is quite square-shaped. People who write in this fashion show an aptitude for construction and mechanical ability (see Figure 11).

Notice how Thomas Edison wrote. Invention of so many diverse devices required acute mechanical and construction ability, which is revealed in this square writing. In addition, those long, strong *t* bars show powerful drive, enthusiasm, will, and determination.

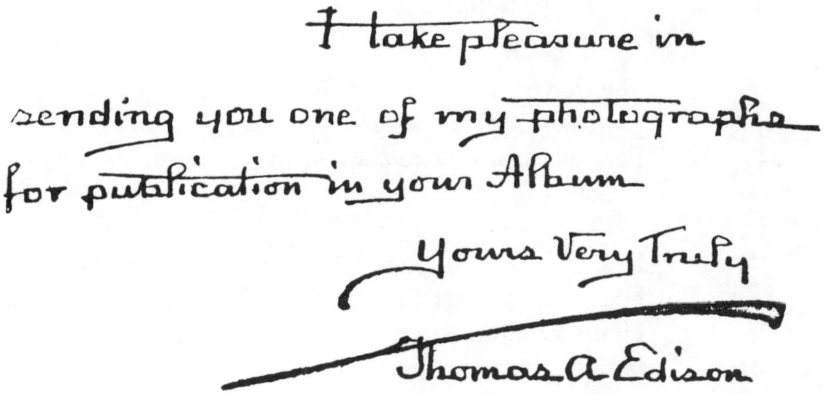

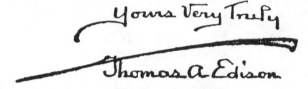

I take pleasure in sending you one of my photographs for publication in your Album

Yours Very Truly

Thomas A Edison

B

FIGURE 33.

The bottom arc in Figure 33 is inflated. Inflation shows vanity. In addition, the underlength extends past the body of the letter itself out to the left. This writer puts himself on a pedestal and thereby calls attention to himself, underlining his own importance. His ego is represented by the capital letter and the pedestal by the extended underlength. Since the bottom arc is inflated, corresponding to the lower zone, this also shows materialism.

FIGURE 34.

In Figure 34, the stroke extends upward. It shows one who is willing to undertake a new project of some kind, though it may be risky. The upstroke appears to be pointing to the heavens, to outer space.

FIGURE 35.

The constant changes in the letter in Figure 35 indicate a hypochondriac. He always feels that there is something wrong with him. Whatever he does is not good enough, and he returns and changes the letter again and again.

FIGURE 36.

The complicated, overdone, ugly letter in Figure 36 shows vulgarity—one who is loud, corresponding to the gaudy letter he produces. He will often be pedantic about trivial details.

FIGURE 37.

The letter in Figure 37 has a sharp top. When a particular part of a letter should be round and instead is pointed, as if it were a knife, we see resentment.

FIGURE 38.

In Figure 38, the pointed (or angular) shape is at the bottom of a letter that would ordinarily be round. As Figure 37 indicates, this shows resentment. In addition, here is a piercing, sharp personality, bent on getting his own way. The angular shape reveals hardness and rigidity, especially when it dips into the lower (physical) zone for some strength.

FIGURE 39.

Figure 39 is a combination of Figures 37 and 38. It is sharp at the top as well as at the bottom and thus shows the same traits. There is no way out, since both sides are angular also; hence, we see a person who will not compromise.

FIGURE 40.

In Figure 40, we see a round beginning stroke. This shows talkativeness in the writer, plus a sense of humor. This extra beginning stroke was not necessary —but it was as if the writer had to tell something to somebody—pull someone over to whisper in his ear.

FIGURE 41.

The end stroke in Figure 41 ascends to the upper zone. It shows imagination and high-mindedness. Many poets write this hand.

FIGURE 42.

The hooks in Figure 42, which are also angular, show stubbornness. As we know, hooks hold on to something: they do not want to let go.

C

FIGURE 43.

Figure 43 shows a personality who seems to be always computing something. Follow the beginning stroke—in, down, around, and over. The writer may be in trouble, but he persists and gets out of it. The shape itself looks like a side view of the human brain.

FIGURE 44.

The angularly shaped letter in Figure 44 shows what an angular shape represents, speed. The writer is quick and usually more intelligent than the round (arcade) writer, so we see intelligence.

D

FIGURE 45.

The letter in Figure 45 is written in two parts. We see the individual standing alone. Since this letter is normally made of connected lines, this technique of writing shows a deficiency in adjusting to what others may do.

FIGURE 46.

The simple letter with an arc at the left, as in Figure 46, shows taste. The writer has a flair for the finer things of life. Try writing this letter. You will feel the grace of it.

FIGURE 47.

The letter in Figure 47 is in the form of a musical note and therefore shows a musical interest.

FIGURE 48.

The upper length extends quite high into the upper zone and shows a moral personality; this is a person who respects spiritual ideals.

FIGURE 49.

The letter is looped, therefore showing vanity. It also shows sensitivity, as if the loops were an added shield of protection from getting hurt.

∂ d̲

8 g̲

Ɛ e̲

FIGURE 50.

The letters *d*, *g*, and *e* as shown in Figure 50, are called the Greek *d*, *g*, and *e*, because they resemble the way those letters are formed in the Greek alphabet. When two or all three of them appear repeatedly in someone's handwriting, it is a sign of culture, of a literary-oriented individual. Such letters are usually found among intellectuals and people with high IQs, and their presence indicates speed and good taste.

If only one of these signs appears—and especially if it is relatively infrequent—we see someone who is trying to appear cultured, but is not quite.

Notice the many Greek *d*'s and *g*'s (also called *figure-8 g*'s) of Victor Hugo (Figure 50B) and Mark Twain (Figure 50A):

FIGURE 50A.

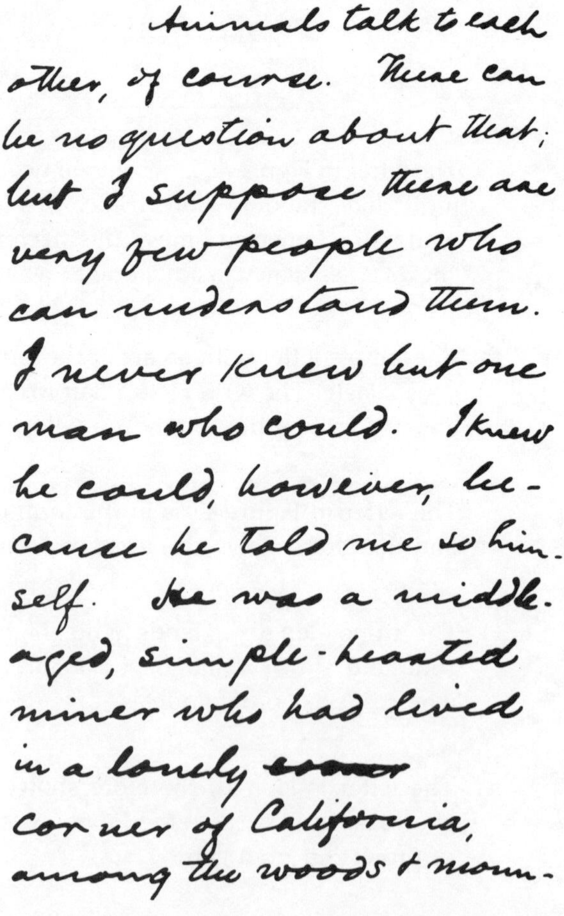

Animals talk to each
other, of course. There can
be no question about that;
but I suppose there are
very few people who
can understand them.
I never knew but one
man who could. I knew
he could, however, be-
cause he told me so him-
self. He was a middle-
aged, simple-hearted
miner who had lived
in a lonely ~~corner~~
cor ner of California,
among the woods & moun-

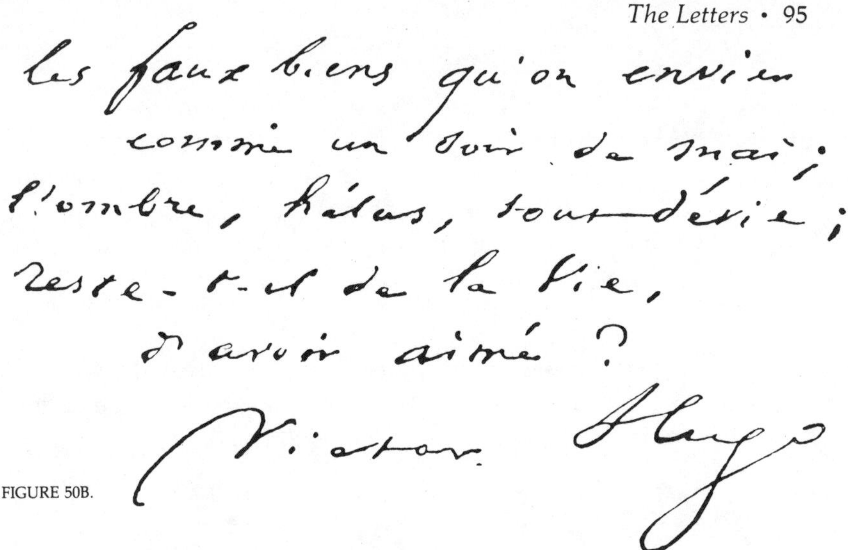

Les faux biens qu'on envie
comme un don de mai;
l'ombre, hélas, tout désire;
reste-t-il de la vie,
d'avoir aimé?

Victor Hugo

FIGURE 50B.

FIGURE 51.

Figure 51 shows pessimism and depression. Its head is turned all the way down, demonstrating the writer's feelings.

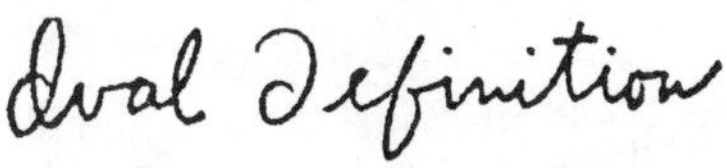

Oval Definition

FIGURE 52.

In Figure 52 we see two different ways of writing the same letter. Wherever this form appears, with any letter, it indicates versatility. In the capital *I*, it hints at someone who is not quite sure who he is, so he tries out different personalities.

FIGURE 53.

When the loop is harmoniously swung around, as in Figure 53, we see one of two things: in a superior script, logic in decision making; in an inferior script, an attempt to use logic that the writer does not possess.

A superior script is one that often contains original letter forms, simplicity, words and lines clearly separated, and usually speedy writing. An inferior script is one that often contains lack of originality, a strong adherence to copybook standard, ostentation, and usually a slow hand, with words and lines often becoming entangled.

There is a nice swing in Figure 53, reflecting the mind's ability to move in whatever direction is necessary.

deduction

FIGURE 54.

In Figure 54, we see that the letters are connected, showing the power of deduction. This writer uses logic, building fact upon fact, just as he places letter upon letter.

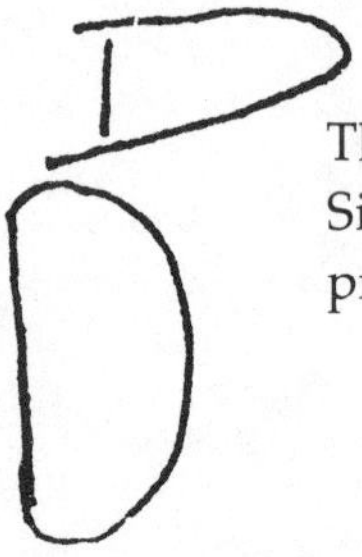

The capital letters in Figure 55 are excessively large. Since the capital letter represents the ego, they show pride, vanity, conceit, and jealousy.

FIGURE 55.

E

FIGURE 56.

The letter in Figure 56 shows a loop, and the letter itself is written in the form of a garland. Garlands indicate friendliness. The round, easy way it is written shows casualness, lightheartedness, even carelessness.

FIGURE 57.

The end stroke in Figure 57 comes up, over, and down the left side, showing someone who distorts facts. Picture the beginning of the end stroke (at the right side of the letter) as the writer's right ear. By the time the stroke has traveled around to where it ends (by the left ear), the story has changed. The true story went in one ear and out the other.

FIGURE 58.

The letter in Figure 58 shows two concave arcs. This capital E looks like two eyes staring at something and it denotes the keen observer.

FIGURE 59.

The beginning stroke in Figure 59 touches the top part of the letter, like a weight of some kind pressing down on it. It shows the writer's difficulty in handling his concerns.

In Figure 60 we have an underlength that would underline the rest of the word. The fashion in which the writer extends this capital (the ego) shows self-admiration.

FIGURE 60.

F

The letter in Figure 61 shows wavy lines, and as we learned from the *t* bar, wavy lines indicate gaiety, a sense of fun, often the practical joker.

FIGURE 61.

When the top stroke extends over the whole word, as it would do in Figure 62, it shows a feeling of protection. This is a masculine quality, but it is found in many women, especially those bringing up children alone.

FIGURE 62.

The simplified strokes in Figure 63 show the writer's urge to speed and a lack of adornment in his personal life-style.

FIGURE 63.

The letter in Figure 64 contains a knot, showing toughness.

FIGURE 64.

See Figure 5. The same explanation holds true here.

FIGURE 65.

In Figure 66 we see a triangular shape with the end stroke horizontal. Angles, as we know, show hardness, and there are three of them here, all in the lower zone. This hints at a strong resistance to interference—absolutely any interference whatsoever. It is probably caused by sexual frustration. (See also Chapter 6, Figure 13).

FIGURE 66.

The letter *G* is discussed in Chapter 5.

H

FIGURE 67.

In Figure 67, we see the downstroke extending under the body of the letter and to the left. This person, because of his stubborn nature, would rather fight than compromise. The stubbornness is demonstrated by the long downstroke, as though he were clouting someone. The fact that he would prefer to fight for his position is shown by the leftward tendency. Not only does he not end the letter with a rightward finishing stroke (which is normal and shows a good relationship to the other person), but he goes the opposite way, leftward. This declares defiantly that he is withdrawing his social attentions from the other person.

Note: If an individual's handwriting tends toward a specific direction in one particular zone, it indicates a strong meaning. Take Figure 67 as an example. This letter shows a vertical writing in general, but a lower zone with a distinct tendency toward the left—reclined writing. This shows that, although the writer maintains a more or less stable posture in his intellectual and everyday life, in matters of sex or money or materialistic pleasures, he effects a certain withdrawal.

FIGURE 68.

The vulgar-looking and ornate letter in Figure 68 has a vertical line added in unnecessarily between the left and right parts. Obviously this writer displays an undue claim of self-importance. Adolf Hitler wrote this way. (Many graphologists believe that the vertical line represented his moustache.)

FIGURE 69.

The upper zone in Figure 69 hardly exists at all. Hence this writer does not believe in spiritual ideals.

FIGURE 70.

The upper zone in Figure 70 is large—four times the size of the middle zone. We see an idealistic, spiritual, and often religious individual.

FIGURE 71.

There is no end stroke in Figure 71, and since the end stroke represents the relationship to one's fellowman, we see meanness here.

The letter *I* is discussed in Chapter 4.

J

FIGURE 72.

In Figure 72, the loop is tremendous and also extends to the left. This writing is found among many male homosexuals. If you notice, the loop is similar to the underlength of the *g* and represents a phallus. The fact that it veers to the left, although the letter itself inclines to the right, shows what reclined writing would show —an opposite role. If the writer is male, we see him playing the female role. The rightward tendency of the other two zones show him to be quite extroverted, the leftward lower zone hints that he is introverted sexually.

Note: It is very difficult for a graphologist to say definitely whether an individual is or is not a homosexual. What he can detect is that the person thinks of himself as sexually unusual. Distortions in the lower zone or strangely shaped letters show a sex life that is of an uncommon sort, but not necessarily homosexuality. Remember, this is what the writer himself feels. The homosexual who doesn't consider homosexuality strange will not reflect this in his writings.

Since the left represents the past (the mother), apparently in the writer's youth, he became confused about the proper role he was to play in life. He rejected the father role and preferred the mother figure, which apparently evidenced more warmth. As an adult, the former child now seeks this same nonviolent warmth.

K

FIGURE 73.

The letter in Figure 73 is split into different parts. It shows someone who lacks adjustment and can be compared to disconnected writing. It is as though, through the spaces where he did not write, intuition of some kind seeped in. The writer is usually quite clever and has many ideas, although he doesn't do things as most other people do (indicated by the unusual splitting of the letter).

FIGURE 74.

The end stroke in Figure 74 turns out to be a downstroke, made with considerable pressure and extended quite deeply into the lower zone. This shows someone on the defensive; he keeps his "hand" at his side instead of reaching out with it. He dips into the lower zone for strength and stresses it. This hints at brutality and stubbornness.

L

FIGURE 75.

The horizontal stroke in Figure 75 is darkened (technically called *shading*). This unbalanced distribution of shading (one area of the letter has it, the others do not), shows poor circulation plus moodiness. This kind of writing often occurs at puberty or menopause. The shaded area created by heavy pressure seems to suggest a physical condition of which the body is aware and to which it responds. Since only the middle zone is heavily pressured, the condition lies somewhere in midbody, probably in the abdominal area.

FIGURE 76.

The letter in Figure 76 looks like a zero and indicates someone with a mathematical bent.

P

L

FIGURE 77.

The downstroke in Figure 77 is severed into two parts. Imagine this letter superimposed over the body of a person. The break would lie somewhere in the area of the heart. Therefore we see a weak heart or one that may be about to have an attack.

/

FIGURE 78.

The letter in Figure 78 is highly simplified, and whenever a letter is simplified and still contains all the parts necessary for reading (as is the case here), we see a quick, sensible mind.

4

FIGURE 79.

The letter in Figure 79 is in the shape of a number 4, showing a love of order and method. The square shape indicates a desire to put things in some kind of order, and the resemblance to a number adds methodicalness.

M

(Note: The letter M is considered one of the most important letters.)

FIGURE 81.

In Figure 80 we have a diagram of the basic letter *M*, consisting of its three humps. The first hump (a) represents the writer's ego; the second hump (b) represents his social status; the third hump (c) represents other people. Should a particular hump not reflect the simple *M*, we look for variations, as we looked for variations from the school model (Palmer Method) and analyzed the deviations.

FIGURE 80.

The letter in Figure 81 shows an arc that curves under the body of the letter. It shows the performer, the speechmaker; the arc looks like an arm making a kind of gesture to the audience.

FIGURE 82.

When only two "tops" (humps) are made, as in Figure 82, the first represents the ego and the second the other person. Since the first part here is higher than the second, we see the writer's ego as of more importance than the other person. He is probably proud and conceited.

FIGURE 83.

In Figure 83 the first part of the letter is lower than the second part, although the whole letter itself mounts toward the end, showing ambition. The writer's ego is lower than the image he has of the other person. This indicates an inferiority complex, one who is dependent on others' opinions.

FIGURE 84.

The letter in Figure 84 is looped, and loops are an attention-getting device. In addition the blown-up size of this letter indicates vanity.

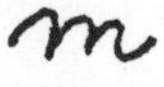

FIGURE 85.

In Figure 85, we have a capital letter that, although it has the opportunity to show off its ego by making itself larger than the rest of the word, doesn't do so. This indicates a writer who is modest, simple, and retiring.

FIGURE 86.

Obviously a letter made in the form of a musical note, as in Figure 86, shows musical interest.

FIGURE 87.

In Figure 87, the starting stroke, instead of beginning from the left, starts from the right, as though the writer needed some extra flourish to communicate his thoughts. We see talkativeness and a good sense of humor here.

FIGURE 88.

In the ugly-looking letter in Figure 88, the middle stroke descends sharply, showing materialism. Its ugly shape indicates vulgarity.

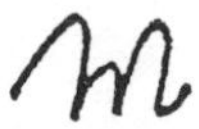

FIGURE 89.

In Figure 89, the middle hump is lower than the other two. Since the second hump shows the social status of the writer, this form implies a dissatisfaction with his social position or his job. People who feel this way tend to rely heavily on public opinion in deciding on a course of action.

FIGURE 90.

In Figure 90 the middle hump is highest of the three. This writer relies more on his own opinion than on that of others. Because the second hump is "climbing" above the first and third, we see an ambitious person who may step on others to attain his goal.

FIGURE 91.

In Figure 91, the letter is written in a wavy fashion, without distinct shape. This shows changeability. A diplomat, who must often evade ticklish situations, might write in this manner.

FIGURE 92.

The letter in Figure 92 is called a thready connection. Making the proper upstrokes and downstrokes was too much trouble for this writer. He takes the easy way out and avoids them all. People who write like this usually find it difficult to make decisions and are prone to lapse into hysteria.

Note: This thready *M* is not to be confused with the thready dying out of a word which implies unwillingness to commit oneself—a subtle difference. (See Chapter 10, Figure 5.)

FIGURE 93.

In Figure 93 the letter is written in the garland form— easygoing, open at the top. The garland betokens a friendly, kind individual, who doesn't conceal how he feels. Its round form shows warmth and softness.

FIGURE 94.

When the angle changes, as it does in Figure 94, we see a person who cannot decide whether he wants to live in the past, present, or future.

When the writing shows only two changes in angle the indecision is not as severe as when the writing changes angles in three directions. Nevertheless, the writer is torn.

FIGURE 95.

In Figure 95 we see a small, crowded *m*. Since the *m* represents so many social aspects of the individual, this letter indicates a narrow-minded person who chooses to crowd himself in. He is probably shy.

FIGURE 96.

This rounded letter in Figure 96 shows someone with a heart of gold. Roundness implies softness, like a bouncing ball, whereas angularity implies hardness, sharpness, like the point of a knife.

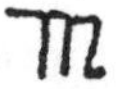

FIGURE 97.

With a letter such as the one in Figure 97, it is a good idea to watch the writer while he writes it. It is possible that he may take his hand off the page and make a nearly conscious decision as to how the letter should be completed. If one goes over the letter without lifting the writing tool, one has to use what are called *covering-up strokes*—the upstroke and the downstroke share the same line. Covering-up strokes indicate that the writer is hiding something. It usually involves cheating in one manner or another, and hence the writer tries to show as little of himself as possible, avoiding separate up-strokes and downstrokes, since separate strokes would show more of his true personality than he wants to reveal.

FIGURE 98.

In Figure 98 the strokes are broken, although there is no doubt that the letter is an *m*. Writing like this is found among frugal persons (as though they were saving by not filling in the entire letter) and among nervous people. The latter seem to need to lift the hand from the page, possibly because it trembles.

FIGURE 99.

The third hump in Figure 99 is the highest of the three. Since the third hump depicts the writer's relationship with other people, this shows envy. He has placed others on a pedestal higher than himself and now begrudges the heights to which they have risen.

FIGURE 100.

In Figure 100, we see the end stroke going to the right and down. Since the normal, social thing would be to extend the final to the right, this downstroke betokens a pessimistic attitude. This writer sulks and probably suffers from depression. His writing is directed downward to reflect his feelings.

FIGURE 101.

The letter in Figure 101 shows tacky elaboration. We see exaggeration (because of the unnecessary strokes) and surely a lack of taste. The letter itself has a crude look about it.

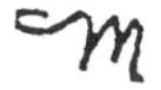

FIGURE 102.

In Figure 102 the beginning stroke is hooked. A hook can reveal egotism, greed, stubbornness. Here the hook represents ego, and because it points inward toward the first hump of the M, it shows selfishness.

FIGURE 103.

The beginning stroke in Figure 103 is both large and flourished. Since the first part of the *m* shows the ego, we see snootiness. The writer is trying to give an exaggerated image of his own worth. When used in an ungraceful manner like this, flourish strokes show false pretense and affectation.

FIGURE 104.

When the various humps are a uniform height, as in Figure 104, we see intelligence, good taste, and a generally amiable disposition. Its similarity to the block letter, which shows simplicity, implies intelligence, and good taste is shown by the very fact that the writer has chosen the simplest possible form. We read good disposition in the equal size of the humps—none distorts the others; social status, ego, and relationship to his fellowman are all in due proportion.

FIGURE 105.

In Figure 105, the end downstroke is significantly lighter than the rest of the letter. This writer has a mean streak in him. He cuts off his relationships with his fellowman (the shortened third hump). In addition, since the light downstroke heads in the direction of the lower (sexual) zone, he probably cannot enjoy sexual relationships in the normal way. The combination of meanness and inability to enjoy normal sex hints that this writer is by nature a sadist. (See Chapter 6.)

FIGURE 106.

The end downstroke in Figure 106 is considerably more lightly written than the rest of the letter. Heading into the lower zone, as it does, the area where the strength of the individual lies, it implies fatigue and weakness.

FIGURE 107.

The endstroke in Figure 107 is written with heavy pressure, indicating brutality. There are two reasons for this: (1) all endstrokes show the writer's relationship to the other person, and (2) the third part of the *m* also shows this. Thus this personality trait is emphasized.

FIGURE 108.

The endstroke in Figure 108 goes up into the upper zone and ends in a dot. The upper zone indicates the imaginative and intellectual aspect of the writer, and the leftward tendency of the stroke reveals negativism about him. (Leftward tendencies often mean negativism and rightward tendencies positivism.) The heavy pressure of the dot shows materialism. Adding up these facts, we conclude that this writer engages in calculating flattery.

FIGURE 109.

The endstroke in Figure 109 is hooked. A hook in general shows tenacity, and when it is found at the end of the *m* (relationship to others), we see someone whose dealings are marked by stubbornness.

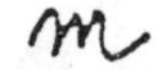

FIGURE 110.

See Chapter 8, Figure 19.

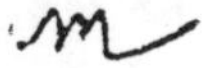

FIGURE 111.

See Chapter 8, Figure 20.

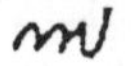

FIGURE 112.

The endstroke in Figure 112 extends into the upper zone (spirituality, mysticism). When this endstroke is found at the last part of the *m* (relationship with other people), we see one who couches his human relationships in religious terms.

N

The letter *n* and the capital *N* are overshadowed, in terms of importance, by the letter *m*. We usually find that the way the writer writes the beginning and the endstrokes of the *n* will be like that of the *m*.

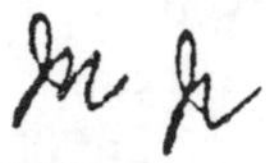

FIGURE 113.

The *m* and *n* shown here (compare Figure 87) have the same form and therefore, the same meaning. The *m* is usually written in the form of an arcade, and likewise the *n*.

O

FIGURE 114.

The letter in Figure 114 is a closed oval and shows a person who is secretive. We will see in a later chapter that the degree of closedness of the oval letters reflects the degree of closedness in the person.

When we use the expression "oval letter," we mean *a*, *o*, the middle zones of *g* and *d*, or any other letter containing an oval shape.

FIGURE 115.

Figure 115 shows a knotted letter, indicating great secrecy. When there is more than one knot or when the oval is "double knotted," the need for privacy is even more powerful. This form often appears in the handwriting of criminals, who obviously lock themselves in with these knots so they will not be found out (they feel). When knotted ovals appear throughout the handwriting, we often find a paranoid personality. This person feels that somebody out there is against him and he must lock himself in for protection.

Naturally, the more closed the ovals, the more introverted the individual. When one makes a knot or loop (especially double ones), it means that the letter was not closed tightly enough for the writer. By going over it he convinces himself that he has plugged all the "leaks."

FIGURE 116.

In Figure 116 we see the open oval—basically the opposite of the closed oval in Figure 114. Its openness at the top indicates talkativeness, sincerity. The writer is not bottled up but is thoroughly extroverted.

We often see reclined (leftward) writing with open ovals. Although reclined writing hints at withdrawal and reserve, there is no contradiction. When such a writer is approached, though by nature reserved, he is nonetheless able to respond. By contrast, the reclined writer with closed ovals is usually unable to come out of his shell at all.

On the other hand, where the writing is inclined (rightward) but the ovals are closed, we see a person who is really warm, but when exposed to certain situations, in public or private, he closes up and does not know what to say. This is not because he is cold—he is merely subject to an unreasoning fear of the particular person or thing with which he is faced. When opened oval-shaped letters at the top appear with inclined writing, we often find the broad-minded individual. This writer is sincere, but it would be advisable not to tell him any important secrets; it is difficult for him to keep confidences. If there are some open and some closed ovals, then he probably can be trusted with a secret, since he knows how to hold his tongue when it's important.

FIGURE 117.

The *o* in Figure 117 really looks like an *e*, but it's not. If you try to copy it, you will see nothing unnecessary in the writing. It has a beginning stroke and an end stroke, and the letter itself inside may pass for an *o*. Unlike the regular *o*, which is usually written in two motions—a counterclockwise swoop, forming a complete circle, followed by an end stroke—this letter is written in a single motion. This writer has a way of avoiding extra effort.

FIGURE 118.

The oval in Figure 118 is open but looped. This writer sets traps. He is also very shrewd. When he opens his mouth (ovals reflect the mouth in shape) and speaks in a way that appears to be open and honest, he is trying to lure you into something. Once you agree, the trap (loops) snaps shut.

P

FIGURE 119.

The letter in Figure 119 is a *p*, although it's hard to recognize out of context. Excluding the beginning stroke, it shows a saving of writing space, since the downstroke doesn't come all the way around to touch the upstroke. This indicates austerity, avoidance of unnecessary embellishment. The open top between the beginning stroke and its connecting upstroke imply talkativeness.

FIGURE 120.

The letter in Figure 120 was made in two arcs, looking as though it were assembled or constructed. Any such form shows creative ability.

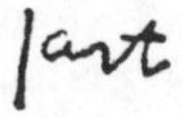

lart

FIGURE 121.

In Figure 121 we see a stroke without the hump and can only read the letter as a *p* by seeing the entire word. This indicates neglectfulness and impatience, possibly forgetfulness, and the speed with which it is written implies liveliness.

V ∧

FIGURE 122.

The letters in Figure 121 are written simply and fast. They often show the quick, brilliant mind, able to solve puzzles rapidly. When simplified writing is combined with quick writing, it is a sign of superior intelligence.

FIGURE 123.

The letter in Figure 123 looks as if it were wearing a top hat. Since this structure reaches into the upper zone, we see an inspirational, idealistic personality.

q

FIGURE 124.

When we see the hump on the wrong side of the stem, as in Figure 124, we obviously have a writer with unusual habits. He is often shy; he places the hump where he feels people won't see it and thus avoids the limelight.

FIGURE 125.

The letter in Figure 125 is written on a base, a pedestal. This shows artistic taste and also draws attention to what the writer has in mind. The base makes the letter into a "drawing," but since it (he feels) is not properly part of the letter, it also indicates a certain degree of falseness in the writer. And, not being necessary, it shows affectation.

Q

The *Q* (*q*), excluding the diagonal bar, has the same interpretation as that of the *o* (without this bar, it is an o). But it is useful to notice changes in pressure in the diagonal bar itself. In most cases, the writer usually lifts his hand and writes the bar as a separate stroke.

FIGURE 126.

In Figure 126 we see the diagonal bar written in much heavier pressure than the body of the letter. As we have seen, heavy pressure shows brutality. Here, it's like a club that is being held over someone's head.

R

FIGURE 127.

The letter in Figure 127 has two loops. Loops show vanity and here indicate an attempt to inflate the writer's image by adding unnecessary extras, as if he were saying, "There is more to me than just this." Two loops hint that the vanity has affected the writer's thinking, perhaps prejudicing it.

FIGURE 128.

The second part of the letter in Figure 128 is lower than the first. This shows curiosity—the first part seems to be looking over the shoulder of the other part. Very often, where this shape of letter occurs, the *i* dot is correspondingly offset (*ι˙*), as if it too wanted to see what was happening.

FIGURE 129.

The letter in Figure 129 looks like a round blob, an unimpressive way of being written. This shows the lazy individual, perhaps a dullard, and since it hasn't a hint of an angle, he possesses no aggressiveness whatsoever.

FIGURE 130.

In Figure 130 we have an *r* that shows strong visual qualities. It resembles the frame of a pair of glasses, its two top points being the eyes. Many people whose eyes are a major factor in their occupation, such as painters, designers, interior decorators (even graphologists), write this broad-structured letter. It also appears often in the writings of people who are considered fancy dressers. The two top parts of the letter can be seen as shoulders and the bottom strokes as perhaps a cape or stole.

S

The letter *s* indicated in Figure 131 resembles the dollar sign, so we know that money is on the writer's mind.

FIGURE 131.

For the letter *T*, please see Chapter 4.

U

The very nature of the letter *u* is a garland, which implies the easygoing, friendly human being. When this natural form is changed—for example, into an angular shape, as in Figure 132—we see a writer with a strong resistance to friendliness. The angle shows hardness in general, and here the hardness is emphasized.

FIGURE 132.

In Figure 133 we see the wavy-lined letter. This writer has the diplomatic touch and tries to be slippery and not commit himself to a particular course of action. Wavy-lined writing also shows versatility.

FIGURE 133.

V

In Figure 134 the word starts off in a connected fashion, and suddenly the *v* rises up and seems to be saying, "I've had enough, let me out of here!" The end of the word is left stranded, alone—a sign of revolt, of one who wants to break away from the conditions as they are.

FIGURE 134.

In Figure 135 there is a hook at the top of the upstroke. The *v* by its very nature, being angular, represents hardness, but that does not seem to be enough for this writer, for he also adds a hook. He is probably mean, the kind of person who seeks revenge for slights. Here he had already finished writing the letter but, having

FIGURE 135.

some unfinished business to tend to, he hooked back onto the end stroke.

W

FIGURE 136.

The letter in Figure 136 has a right to be angular (as does the *v*), but its simplified form shows intelligence and its angularity a piercing mind.

X

FIGURE 137.

The *x* naturally looks like a tough letter, as though two men were dueling with swords. When, as in Figure 137, the end stroke extends an already belligerent letter into the lower zone (to pick up some strength) we see a person with a fierce temper.

FIGURE 138.

In Figure 138 we have two separate strokes crossing each other. The *x* shows a fighting nature when it is written in two strokes that are diagonals. The fact that the strokes cross in the middle shows exactness.

Note: An *x* made in the cursive fashion like this 𝒳 does not show a fighting nature—that is only indicated when the strokes are made as diagonals.

Y

FIGURE 139.

The letter in Figure 139 is made in a soft manner (resembling the Palmer Method, which is by nature a round kind of writing). Any letter with a gentle loop in the lower zone shows friendliness and kindness in relation to the writer's physical drive.

Z

FIGURE 140.

In Figure 140 the end stroke descends when it should be horizontal. This shows that the writer finds himself in a state of depression.

Each of the foregoing letters has something different in its form and, therefore, in the interpretation to be put upon it. Often the same meaning can be derived from several different letters in one person's handwriting. This is because the same characteristic form can appear in different letters. The reader should now be able to discern the meaning of any letter simply by knowing which form it should fit into.

Here are two examples of how it works:

See Figure 8, the letter *A*: -*A* . This letter shows two factors that we are concerned about. It is a capital, and it is quite thin. The capital letter reflects the ego of the writer, and because he "thins himself out," we say that he is shy. The same interpretation would be true of, say, a capital *H*: -*H* . This thin capital also implies that the writer is shy.

In Figure 28, we have a lowercase *a*: *a* . Here the bottom is open, and the letter is oval-shaped. So the rule that applies here applies to any oval-shaped letter with an open bottom— *n* —perhaps the letter *o*: *o* . The letters *a* and *o* are both middle-zone letters, but upper-zone and lower-zone letters also belong to this category, providing that they have round parts in the middle zone; for example, the letter *d*: *d* .

Once you understand the principles, it should be easy to interpret all the possible variations in letter shapes.

15

The Personality Traits

What the graphologist is really seeking in analyzing handwriting are the writer's personality traits. A personality trait is usually composed of many different factors.

For example, if the writing indicated a lack of self-control, passion, impulsiveness, and violence, the graphologist would sum up the personality trait as temper. Should self-control, passion, and violence be present, without impulsiveness, temper would still be indicated, but if violence were the missing element, the graphologist would hesitate to say flat out that the writer has a bad temper. He might admit, however, that the possibility of temper exists.

A similar situation exists in interpreting letters. Before the graphologist weighs the form of a letter into a total analysis, he looks for consistency. In other words, he must find the same form often enough in the writing to be significant before he includes its meaning in the total analysis. Here is the usual rule of thumb: If all the major components are present, we say that the personality trait most definitely exists. If all the major components but one are found, there is a strong possibility that the personality trait exists. If only one major component is found, the writer has a tendency toward this trait.

Absentmindedness

When the *t* bars and the *i* dots (or *j* dots or the cross on the *x*) are usually missing, we see an absentminded person.

I can't understand why I keep forgetting my keys

Adaptability

Garland writing *I can live anywhere* (Chapter 11, Figure 2.)

Round (curved) writing (Chapter 14, Figure 139.)

I'm sure we'll do fine

Moderate-sized capitals (a bit higher than other letters)

David, Carl & I can change our plans

Aesthetic taste

Graceful (harmonious) curves (Chapter 11, Figures 1 and 2.)

I love being in the woods

Greek *d*'s and figure-8 *g*'s (Chapter 14, Figure 50.)

This garden party is a great idea!

Printed capitals (Chapter 14, Figure 3.)

Both Danny & I enjoy art

Affection

Round writing (Chapter 14, Figure 136.)

I love being next to you

Inclined writing   *(Chapter 2, angle AF.)*

I bought a teddy bear for your birthday

Garland writing   *(Chapter 11, Figure 2.)*

Martin misses me

Aggressiveness

Angular   *(Chapter 11, Figure 3.)*

Hey, lets go ahead

Heavy writing   *(Chapter 12, Figure 2.)*

lets get outta here

t bars thin and long (usually descending)   *(Chapter 4, Figure 8, accentuated.)*

meet you in ten minutes

Return stroke of lower loops to the right (instead of to the left.)

Throw it to any guy besides Danny

Speedy writing

I'll race the both of you without shoes

Agreeableness

Garland writing   *(Chapter 11, Figure 2.)*

anything you want, honey

Light writing   *(Chapter 12, Figure 1.)*

I believe you're right

Alcoholism

Descending base line   *(Chapter 7, Figure 3.)*

I need a drink real bad

Pasty writing   *(Chapter 6, Figure 27.)*

If you give me a dime, I'll buy a coffee

Shaky writing

Those were the days my friend

Altruism

Large writing

Can I help you ?

Round writing   *(Chapter 14, Figure 139.)*

let me give you a hand

Legible writing

I would like to assist you

v covering the rest of the word   *(Compare Chapter 4, Figure 31.)*

Very well done Vera

Return stroke of lower loops going to the right (instead of left.)

I'm giving that guy a hand

Ambition

Ascending base line   *(Chapter 7, Figure 2.)*

I took the test to get a promotion

Ascending *t* bars   (Chapter 4, Figure 21.)

I'll talk to your tomorrow about plans

Large capitals   (Chapter 14, Figure 55.)

Yankee Stadium, I'm comin'!

Amiability
Inclined writing   (Chapter 2, angle AF.)

Hi sweetie, wanna meet for lunch?

Round writing   (Chapter 14, Figure 136.)

I'd love to meet you for lunch

Garland writing   (Chapter 11, Figure 2.)

I miss you Jenny

Anger
Angular writing   (Chapter 11, Figure 3.)

get over here!

Pointed *t* bars (at end)   (Chapter 4, Figure 19.)

I can't stand the sight of you

Ungraceful writing   (Chapter 7, Figure 5.)

Don't come back again!!

Arrogance

Large capitals   *(Chapter 14, Figure 55.)*

I despise you... I mean you 9 Henny!

First stroke (hump) of *m* very high   *(Chapter 14, Figure 82.)*

my father makes your father look like my mother

Argumentativeness

Uneven spacing

*Regardless of what you say I disagree
As long as I've known you, you've never made sense*

Totally disconnected writing   *(Chapter 10, Figure 3.)*

I see no logic in your statement

Letters and words connected   *(Chapter 10, Figure 4.)*

It's none of your business !

Initial hooks on beginning strokes   *(Chapter 9, Figure 3.)*

I have one interest in being friendly with you

Artificiality

Large (often ornamented) capitals   *(Chapter 14, Figure 84.)*

Dear Parent Teachers Association —

Large triangular lower loops   *(Chapter 6, Figure 13.)*

Everybody is lovely

Artistic taste
Wide spacing

I love the outdoors

Very wide margins

I love drawing on the mountain

Thin capitals   (Chapter 14, Figure 8.)

Hardly a day passes without Bill + I painting

Garland writing   (Chapter 11, Figure 2.)

This is my painting

Assertiveness
Open ovals   (Chapter 14, Figure 116.)

I've got something on my chest to tell you

Descending *t* bars   (Chapter 4, Figure 8.)

I'm getting out of here

Very tall capitals   (Chapter 14, Figure 55.)

N.Y.C. Here I come!

Abrupt (club shaped or very heavy) end strokes   (Chapter 9, Figure 14.)

I'm running for office in June

Athletic type
Heavy writing   *(Chapter 12, Figure 2.)*

Hey, throw it over here!

Very long lower loops   *(Chapter 6, Figure 9.)*

He's a great football player

Bashfulness
Very light writing   *(Chapter 12, Figure 1.)*

I'm afraid of the dark

Low capitals   *(Chapter 14, Figure 85.)*

I was born in N.Y.C.

Weak (light) end strokes descending to the right   *(Chapter 9, Figure 11.)*

I'm alone because I'm afraid

Bravery
End strokes ascending to the right   *(Chapter 9, figure 14, without the thickening)*

I'll do it alone

Heavy (or very heavy) pressure   *(Chapter 12, Figure 2.)*

I'll take them all on myself!

Broad-mindedness
Very wide spacing (with open ovals)

I've learned a considerable amount on my travels through Eastern Africa

---

Brusqueness

Very large middle-zone letters (Chapter 3, Figure 8.)

Hey you, give me a hand!

Heavy pressure (Chapter 12, Figure 2.)

Get outta my sight

Tall capitals (Chapter 14, Figure 55.)

I Sir Louis Stone, give you 3 hours to leave London!

Brutality

End strokes thickening (Chapter 9, Figure 14.)

I'll flatten you man!

t bar thin at beginning and thick (Chapter 4, Figure 23.,
(or club-shaped) at ending *not necessarily descending*)

Shut up hot shot

Reclined writing (Chapter 2, angles AC or AB.)

Take your things & leave!

Business ability

Inclined writing (Chapter 2, angles AE or AF.)

Can you use a beautiful vacuum cleaner? I just happen......

Very wide spacing

my secretary informed me of your recent merger. Good luck!

Fast writing

I can get it for you wholesale

Business ability

Connected writing   *(Chapter 10, Figure 1.)*

[handwriting sample: It's a pleasure doing business with you]

Words connected

[handwriting sample: Dont forget if it goes down buy and if it goes up sell]

Angular writing   *(Chapter 11, Figure 3.)*

[handwriting sample: I have no time to discuss it with you any longer]

Calmness

Even pressure   *(Chapter 12, Figure 3.)*

[handwriting sample: I feel quite collective these days]

Slow, curved writing

[handwriting sample: I think a weekend by the lake would be just fine]

t bars and i dots placed low   *(Chapter 4, Figure 27.)*

[handwriting sample: my blood pressure is quite steady]

Simplified writing, no long end strokes   *(Chapter 9, Figure 18.)*

[handwriting sample: its wonderful being on vacation with you]

Carefulness

t bars and i dots placed exactly   *(Chapter 4, Figure 1.)*
                                                                     (Chapter 5, Figure 8.)

[handwriting sample: I enjoy detailed work.]

Even pressure, legible writing (*Chapter 12, Figure 3.*)

*I put 2 stamps on just
to make sure*

Even margins (*Chapter 8, Figure 6.*)

*the books are all
quite up to date
as of this morning*

Ovals closed (*Chapter 14, Figure 114.*)

*Though I drive quite slowly,
I use my seat belts*

Carelessness

Omitted *i* dots and *t* bars (*Chapter 5, Figure 19.*)
  (*Chapter 4, Figure 13.*)

Didn't I lend you my jacket?

Uneven pressure

I don't need any mirrors in my car

Irregular spacing

*I'm not gonna fix the roof
rain isn't gonna seep through it I bet the*

Speedy writing

*Doc, I ran so fast I forgot to bring my
wife who is about to give birth!*

Cautiousness

Vertical writing   *(Chapter 2, angle AD.)*

Don't sign until your read it thoroughly

Ovals closed   *(Chapter 14, Figure 114.)*

closed windows stop bugs from coming in

Slow writing   *(Chapter 11, Figure 1.)*

what did you say your name was?

t bars and *i* dots preplaced   *(Chapter 4, Figure 3.)*

without the keys, you do not get the rent

Accentuated punctuation

I'm sure I saw that guy following you !!!
Do you think I'd make such a story up ? ? ? ?

Ceremoniousness

Large capitals (flourished or inflated)   *(Chapter 14, Figure 55.)*

I love being in @hiladelphia

Large writing

How do you like my new gown Sid?

Clannishness (sometimes to the point of bigotry)

Microscopic writing

(I only associate with white Anglo-Saxon Americans)

Lower-zone stroke extended to the left

(Lower-zone strokes extended to the left show sexual repression)

I'm changing my address because my neighbors aren't white

Clearheadedness

Simple distribution of space and even pressure   *(Chapter 12, Figure 3.)*

after we draw up the plans, will start on the plans

Legible and connected writing   *(Chapter 10, Figure 1.)*

If we meet his price, he'll give us the merchandise

Coarseness

Ungraceful writing

It's your turn to take out the garbage!

Ink-filled (pasty, blotchy) especially lower loops

my dog does better work than you do!

Club-shaped end strokes

Take a bath, you stink!

Coldheartedness

Very reclined writing   *(Chapter 2, angle falling between AC and AB.)*

Stay out in the street

Coldheartedness

Angular writing   *(Chapter 11, Figure 3.)*

I feel nothing for you anymore

Descending end strokes heavy and pointed   *(Chapter 9, Figure 14.*
                                                                       pointed and downward)

Forget about the bullets, just march

Abrupt end strokes   *(Chapter 9, Figure 17.)*

I can't stand looking at you anymore

Conceit

Flourishes (especially in signature)

Joe Brown

Large capitals   *(Chapter 14, Figure 55.)*

I love being in London!

Blown-up upper and lower loops   *(Chapter 13, Figure 4.)*
                                                                  (Chapter 6, Figures 9 and 10.)

I can lift 200 pounds in one hand

Signature underscored

Samuel Conlala

First hump of *m* higher than other humps   *(Chapter 14, Figure 82.)*

My dear man, you're in my way!

Concentration

Small middle zone   *(Chapter 3, Figure 4.)*

I am a scientist by profession

i dots and *t* bars low placed   *(Chapter 4, Figure 27.)*

I must finish this work by nightfall

Short lower strokes (sometimes short upper strokes)

I'm sure a queen is worth two bishops

i dots and *t* bars exactly placed   *(Chapter 4, Figure 1.)*

after we divide, we get the quotient

No loops in lower zone   *(Chapter 6, Figure 3.)*

Studying lately is getting easier

Confusion

Words and lines tangling

I think it would be a great idea to go out we'll all have a great time + I'm sure the kids will appreciate it. It isn't always that we get such an opportunity! Hey! wait a minute! I just remembered I have to go to work tomorrow, boy I wish I could make up my mind!

Conscientiousness
Legible writing, level base line   *(Chapter 7, Figure 1.)*

Before I can decide, I need all the facts

Open ovals   *(Chapter 14, Figure 116.)*

I did call that mommy crshed

i dots round and exactly placed   *(Chapter 5, Figure 8.)*

I lived at home till the day I married

Constructiveness
Square-shaped letters (often printed)   *(Chapter 14, Figure 11.)*

I built that building all by myself

Contrariness
Ascending (long) beginning strokes   *(Chapter 9, Figure 4.)*

I should have never married him

Reclined writing   *(Chapter 2, angle AC.)*

Whatever they say I'll disagree to it.

Conventionality
Palmer Method (adherence to school form)   *(writing similar to Chapter 14, Figure 139.)*

I do ever thing I'm told to

Courage
Base line descending at start and then straightening out

Through perseverance we made it

Heavy pressure   *(Chapter 12, Figure 2.)*

I'll take him by myself

Long, strong *t* bars

Just two more miles + we got it

Cowardice
Very light writing   *(Chapter 12, Figure 1.)*

please dont hit me

Weak descending end strokes to the right   *(Chapter 9, Figure 11.)*

I'm afraid hell hurt me

Weak *t* bars

I'm afraid to talk to him

Creative ability
High upper-zone strokes   *(Chapter 14, Figure 70.)*

I love to tinker

Printed letters

I put it together by myself

Greek *d*   *(Chapter 14, Figure 50.)*

*I did the creation with a little
help from my friends*

Connected (or almost always connected) writing   *(Chapter 10, Figure 1.)*

*our new creation has
just been patented*

Creative ability
Wide spacing

We're just finished creating — new line of summarian

Very small writing

my new projects are quite unsuccessful

Cruelty
Heavy pressure and pasty writing   *(Chapter 12, Figure 4.)*

get out and stay out

i dots and *t* bars heavy and pointed   *(Chapter 4, Figure 19.)*

if you think I need you, you're nuts

Downward pointed terminals   *(Chapter 9, Figure 17*
                                                    extended lower.)

you're the ugliest thing I've ever seen

Angular writing   *(Chapter 11, Figure 3.)*

don't come back again!

i dots like arrows   *(Chapter 5, Figure 17.)*

I'll keep William, you live by yourself!

Club-shaped end strokes (ascending/descending)   *(Chapter 9, Figure 14.)*

I'm not gonna warn you again

Long heavy *t* bars (often descending)   *(Chapter 4, Figure 8*
                                                    done heavier.)

Take your clothes and split

Claw-shaped end strokes in signature

William Bell (handwritten signature)

Cunning
Knotted ovals *(Chapter 14, Figure 31.)*

I'm doing this only for you (handwritten)

Thready connection *(Chapter 11, Figure 4.)*

(handwritten thready sample)

Size of small letters frequently changing in size

at this pria I'm actually losing money (handwritten)

Heavy pressure *(Chapter 12, Figure 2.)*

If I wanted you to know what it was would I have put it in a bag? (handwritten)

Angular writing *(Chapter 11, Figure 3.)*

You think you're a wit, but you're only half right! (handwritten)

Deceitfulness
Wavy base line *(Chapter 7, Figure 5.)*

How could you go wrong? 3 for $5.00 5 for $10.00 (handwritten)

Double looped ovals *(Chapter 14, Figure 31 with two loops.)*

you're the only girl in my life Sarah, honestly (handwritten)

Ovals opened at bottom *(Chapter 14, Figure 28.)*

Don't worry, I deposited all the money on friday (handwritten)

Defiance

Open ovals at the left side   *(Chapter 14, Figure 29.)*

I dare the cops to come into my house

Second part of "v" heads upward   *(Chapter 14, Figure 134.)*
and separates from the rest
of the word

If I have to, I'll leave all of you!

Dependability

Ovals at top sometimes closed   *(Chapter 14, Figures 114 and 116.)*

all your things are safe here

Inclined writing   *(Chapter 2 between angles AE and AF.)*

Is there anything I can do for you?

Straight base line   *(Chapter 7, Figure 1.)*

I'll be there at 5.00 P.M. just as planned

Determination

Heavy pressure (especially on *t* bars)   *(Chapter 4, Figure 1.)*

my mind's made up & that's that!

Abrupt end strokes   *(Chapter 9, Figure 17.)*

I'm sure I'll get the position

Angular writing   *(Chapter 11, Figure 3.)*

I'll never give up!

Depression

Descending base line *(Chapter 7, Figure 3.)*

I don't feel good about myself lately

Low *t* bar *(Chapter 4, Figure 27.)*

I can't make anything of myself

Descending signature

martin Sholshi

Diplomat

Closed ovals *(Chapter 14, Figure 114.)*

we'll work it all out

Vertical writing *(Chapter 2, angle AD.)*

I have 2 more years in congress

Middle zone diminishing in size *(Chapter 11, Figure 5.)*
toward the final part of the words

Just sign on the dotted line

Directness

Simplified writing

I'll send it to you immediately

t bar post placed *(Chapter 4, Figure 2.)*

I'll get right to it

No beginning strokes *(Chapter 9, Figure 2.)*

what can I do for you?

Dishonesty

Figures that can be mistaken for other figures

3 (3 or 5?)   4 (6 or 4?)   9 (9 or 2?)

8 (8 or 0?)   1 (1 or 2?)

Wavy base line   (Chapter 7, Figure 5.)

I've never seen him before in my life!

Pasty writing   (Chapter 12, Figure 4.)

I love you with all my heart & soul

Weak or no *t* bars   (Chapter 4, Figure 13.)

I'm positive that I pay you back

Threadlike dying out of words   (Chapter 11, Figure 5.)

I'll pay you within three hours

Opened ovals at the bottom   (Chapter 14, Figure 28.)

I already mailed your our check this morning

Looped (especially double looped) ovals   (Chapter 14, Figure 31.)

I don't owe you a cent

Missing letters

*my secretary notified you last week
about our not receiving any merchandise*

Finesse

Small letters tapering toward end of words   (Chapter 11, Figure 5.)

its so nice of you to help out Joan

Thready connection   *(Chapter 11, Figure 4.)*

I am the north Dhotal

Fussiness

Exact punctuation   *(Chapter 4, Figure 1.)*
                                                     (Chapter 5, Figure 8.)

I want the steak done for exactly twenty eight minutes

i dots like dashes   *(Chapter 5, Figure 17.)*

Just do it the way I want it

Gaiety

Wavy *t* bar   *(Chapter 4, Figure 24.)*

It's time we took a better look at ourselves, where's my contacts?

Large writing

I like you

Large middle-zone letters   *(Chapter 3, Figure 8.)*

I love work, I can sit and watch it for hours

Inclined writing   *(Chapter 2, angles AE–AF.)*

I got the keys, now all I need is a car

Ascending base line   *(Chapter 7, Figure 2.)*

I had a great year with your last week

Gluttony

Coarse, ugly capitals   *(Chapter 14, Figure 68.)*

I want more chicken!

Pasty writing   *(Chapter 12, Figure 4.)*

*no motta what I eat, its
never enough*

Humility

Low, simple capitals   *(Chapter 14, Figure 85.)*

my name is alice brown

Pretended humility

Capital letter *I* low, but letter *i* high

I don't think I will qualify for the job

Humor

Wavy *t* bars   *(Chapter 4, Figure 24.)*

t b or not t b, that is congestion

"Crack the whip" *t* bars

Consumption be done about it

Comma ("laughing mouth") *i* dots   *(Chapter 5, Figure 18.)*

of cough it can

Signature with wavy or curved line underneath

Lany Smith

Hypocrisy

Opened ovals at bottom   *(Chapter 14, Figure 28.)*

I've never seen your before in my life

Reclined writing   *(Chapter 2 between angles AC and AB.)*

Do as I say not as I do

Closed, knotted ovals   *(Chapter 14, Figure 31.)*

Honesty is the best policy - really

Incredulity

Capitals very thin or narrow at the base in comparison to the top

I do not trust David or George, whatever they say

Intelligence

Figure 8 g's   *(Chapter 5, Figure 22.)*

Studying in College is a breeze

i dots and *t* bars joining following letters   *(Chapter 5, Figure 13.)*

People only truly learn by their experiences

Simplified and quick writing

Obtaining my Ph.D was relatively

High upper extensions and small middle zones

I'm very satisfied with my progress in scientific work -

Jealousy

Incurving *t* bar   *(Chapter 4, Figure 20.)*

Look at that deposit he just made!

Incurving hooks   *(Chapter 9, Figure 16.)*

It doesn't bother me at all if he goes out with her

Very large initial capitals   *(Chapter 14, Figure 55.)*

I envy no man

High-flying *t* bars   *(Chapter 4, Figure 2.)*
(The *t* bar should be high and away from the stem)

I don't care what he has

Luxury
Very widely spaced

Three cars + a summer home, that's life!

Left margin widening   *(Chapter 8, Figure 3.)*

I don't seem to know what happened to all of our money

Wide right margin   *(Chapter 8, Figure 1.)*

I have no responsibilities

Very large writing

I love the life of Riley

Large lower-zone letters   (Chapter 3, Figure 5.)

I love vacationing with you honey

Materialism
Muddy (heavy) *i* dots   (Chapter 5, Figure 16.)

it's not too expensive for my tastes

Inflated lower loops   (Chapter 3, Figure 5B.)

Though I have many others, I simply must have that pocketbook

Heavy-pressured writing   (Chapter 12, Figure 2.)

I get time & half for my overtime

Mathematical aptitude
Capital letters figure-shaped   (Chapter 6, Figure 2.)

Government leaders, such as Queen Dorothy have asked the French government have asked for assistance

---

Memory
i dots and *t* bars placed exactly   (Chapter 5, Figure 8.)
                                                               (Chapter 4, Figure 1.)

I paid exactly $23.76 on May 3, 1976, for the wristwatch which is in your locker now.

Mental Activity

Ascending base line (*Chapter 7, Figure 2.*)

Theoretically this formula is correct

Simplified (nonflourished) writing (*Chapter 14, Figure 3.*)

we dress casually

t bars postplaced (*Chapter 4, Figure 2.*)

I can't wait to get started

Miserliness

Hooked writing (*Chapter 9, Figure 10.*)

It costs twenty six cents, sos make sure I get the change

Very small, cramped writing

I eat very little, so I can save money

Exact punctuation (*Chapter 4, Figure 1.*)
(*Chapter 5, Figure 8.*)

I walk 6 six miles everyday to save eighty cents on carfare.

Modesty

Small capitals (*Chapter 14, Figure 85.*)

I don't know why george t allen should pick me

Simplified writing (*Chapter 5, Figure 3.*)

Dear joe, we we want are looking forward to your visiting our humble abode   David

---

Musical taste

Garland writing *(Chapter 11, Figure 2.)*

"Money Money" is my favorite song

Very large middle-zone letters *(Chapter 3, Figure 8.)*

I love playing the drums

Inclined writing *(Chapter 2, angles AE–AF.)*

whenever you play, my heart skips a beat

Narrow-mindedness

Very small, cramped writing *(Chapter 14, Figure 95.)*

No matter who wins, I'll always vote Republican

Nervousness

Frequently changing slant *(Chapter 14, Figure 94.)*

I've been so on edge lately it's terrible

m strokes broken *(Chapter 14, Figure 98.)*

its My own fault that My arms are'nt steady

Wavy base line *(Chapter 7, Figure 5.)*

my chiropractor gives me great rubdowns for tension

Shaky connections

Can you really blame me for being on edge

Nervousness
Illegibility

my nerves are really shot

Nonconformity
Change of slant (Chapter 14, Figure 94.)

I do as I please regardless of whatever others may want, wish

Large (usually angular) writing (Chapter 11, Figure 3.)

I'll always be a revolutionary

Large "strange" capitals (Chapter 5, Figure 1.)

I don't care what society thinks I gonna live on a mountain.

Observation
First stroke of *r* higher than second (Chapter 14, Figure 128.)

I remember what she wore yesterday

Concave arcs (Chapter 14, Figure 58.)

Everyday, Eddie + I use our telescopes to view the heavens

i dots made like an arc open at the right side (Chapter 5, Figure 15.)

It's obvious you haven't eaten in a while, your tongue is all white

Exact punctuation (Chapter 4, Figure 1.)
(Chapter 5, Figure 8.)

There were 3 couples, 2 with 2 children and everyone wore pants, except for the youngest woman who wore a full length dress.

Obstinacy

"Whiplash" *t* bar   (*Chapter 4, Figure 16.*)

I'm not moving from this place!

t bars hooked   (*Chapter 4, Figure 17.*)

I won't budge two feet till you apologize to me

t bars down and curved

I'll never speak to Beth again

t bars descending with heavy pressure   (*Chapter 4, Figure 8.*)

Let her change first then I will

Optimism

Ascending base line   (*Chapter 7, Figure 2.*)

I feel great these days

t bars ascending   (*Chapter 4, Figure 21.*)

I lost a lot of weight + I feel great

Left margin widens as it descends   (*Chapter 8, Figure 3.*)

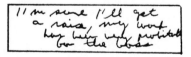

Ascending signature

Paul Brown

Perserverance

Concave lines

Beginnings are difficult for me, but once I start, I get the job done

Angular writing   (Chapter 11, Figure 3.)

I never let anything get in my way

Very long *t* bars (showing determination)

It took me twenty years to build up this business — from scratch now look at it !

Perspicuity

Connected writing   (Chapter 10, Figure 1.)

Let me make myself perfectly clear

Angular writing   (Chapter 11, Figure 3.)

I speak straight to the point

Very small middle zone

I neither added nor subtracted a thing

Pessimism

Descending base line   (Chapter 7, Figure 3.)

There's just no hope for me anymore

Last word suddenly drops

I know I'll never be successful

Physical Activity
Firm downstrokes   *(See Chapter 6, Figure 22.)*

If you catch this you're in the game

Speedy writing

Ted I'll catch you later

Angular writing   *(See Chapter 11, Figure 3.)*

I send over the plate, not first

Poetic taste
"Lasso" loops

a word I spoke, some heart it broke
'Twas just a word, but oh 'Twas heard

Prejudice
Completely angular writing   *(Chapter 11, Figure 3.)*

I hate anyone who's not White

Procrastination
i dots and *t* bars preplaced   *(Chapter 5, Figure 7.)*
                                                     (Chapter 4, Figure 3.)

I'll do it tomorrow, don't worry about it

Slow writing   *(Chapter 11, Figure 1.)*

If I can do it tomorrow,
why should I do it today?

Pugnacity

Abrupt finals (especially on *m*)   *(Chapter 9, Figure 17.)*

Sam, I'm through with you

Ascending club-shaped end strokes   *(Chapter 9, Figure 14.)*

you give me the creeps

Pointed end strokes

leave me alone, will ya

Heavy *i* dots   *(Chapter 5, Figure 16.)*

O is joy is ichy

t bars and end strokes very heavy   *(Chapter 9, Figure 14.)*

I can't stand looking at you

t bars heavy and descending   *(Chapter 4, Figure 8.)*

I hated you from the first

Quarrelsomeness

i dots like dashes   *(Chapter 5, Figure 17.)*

I'd rather fight it out than ague

Hooks   *(Chapter 9, Figure 16.)*

Lets him come to me first

Heavy pressure   *(Chapter 12, Figure 2.)*

who cares what you think

Uneven spacing

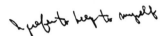

Refinement
Small light writing (with *i* dots quite high and light)   *(Chapter 12, Figure 1.)*

Reserve
Reclined writing   *(Chapter 2, angles AC–AB.)*

Ovals closed and/or looped   *(Chapter 14, Figure 114.)*

Very short *t* bars

Resistance
Heavy hooked *t* bars   *(Chapter 4, Figure 17.)*

Heavy *t* bars

Angular writing   *(Chapter 11, Figure 3.)*

Resistance

Heavy pressure   *(Chapter 12, Figure 2.)*

His offer doesn't move me

Very reclined writing   *(Chapter 2, angle AB.)*

just leave me out of it

Sarcasm

i dots like arrows   *(Chapter 5, Figure 17.)*

Hey beauty, not you shipwreck

Angular (or pointed) bottoms   *(Chapter 14, Figure 38.)*

Hey you look gruñt, gotta new job?

Secretiveness

Ovals closed, knotted and double knotted   *(Chapter 14, Figure 115.)*
                                                                   (Chapter 14, Figure 31.)

I prefer to tell as little as I know

Very reclined writing   *(Chapter 2, angle AB.)*

I always keep my mouth shut

Self-confidence

Line underscoring signature

Joe Black

Large (unflourished) signature

Dave Green

Self-control

Level base line   *(Chapter 7, Figure 1.)*

Though he raised his hands to me, I simply ignored him.

Vertical writing   *(Chapter 2, angle AD.)*

I lost ten pounds on my diet already

Size of letters even

The doctor told me I have normal blood pressure

Legible writing

I simply avoid the bakery & the donuts don't bother me

Convex *t* bars   *(Chapter 4, Figures 4 and 5.)*

We've saved, not splurged, now will be able to buy that new car

---

Selfishness

End stroke of signature circling over, enclosing name

Joe

Signature both overlined and underlined

Joe

Capitals (beginning and/or ending) with hooks

Regardless of who's around, I come first - God remember that!

Beginning strokes inturned   *(Chapter 9, Figure 3.)*

Let them call wait, I'm hungry!

Selfishness

Very reclined writing

(Chapter 2, angles AC–AB.)

I gotta take care of me & nobody else

Angular writing

(Chapter 11, Figure 3.)

I bought three sodas, all for myself

Self-protectiveness

Signature with line covering it

Henry

Signature ending enclosing it

(Chapter 9, Figure 9.)

Self-satisfaction

Signature end stroke underlining it

Brown

Tall capitals

(Chapter 14, Figure 55.)

I've reaped considerably from my toil

Large writing

I've always had a feeling of accomplishment

Sensitivity

d with looped stem

(Chapter 14, Figure 53.)

From childhood, I've always been "touchy"

Star-shaped *t* bar

I hope she didn't notice that I stutter

(Mature) disconnected writing

my feelings get hurt easily

Inclined writing   (Chapter 2 between angles AE and AF.)

I start to squirm when anyone speaks about nuals

Sensuousness

Inflated lower loops   (Chapter 3, Figure 5A.)

I just love looking at you

Pasty "muddy" looking writing

I had 4 steaks, 3 casseroles + then a glass of tea + I threw up, I knew I shouldn't have had that tea

Inclined (or very inclined) writing   (Chapter 2, angles AE–AF.)

I just look at you + my passion flairs up!

Sentimentality

Very inclined writing   (Chapter 2, angle AF.)

I really miss the good old days

Unnecessary punctuations and underlining

I saw this teddy bear! I just had to buy it! It reminded me so much of you. You can understand, right??

Shrewdness

Wavy writing—thinning out toward end (Chapter 11, Figure 5.)

[handwriting sample]

Sincerity

Ovals open (Chapter 14, Figure 116.)

[handwriting sample]

Inclined writing (Chapter 2, angle AE.)

[handwriting sample]

Straight base line (and legibility) (Chapter 7, Figure 1.)

[handwriting sample]

Slyness

Knotted ovals (Chapter 14, Figure 31.)

[handwriting sample]

Crooked base line (Chapter 7, Figure 4.)

[handwriting sample]

Snobbishness

Capital *P* very tall and artificial writing

[handwriting sample]

First stroke (hump) of *m* higher than others (Chapter 14, Figure 82.)

[handwriting sample]

Triangular lower loops

I've done more with my life than any of you

Very wide left margin *(Chapter 8, Figure 2.)*

I only go out with college graduates like myself

Sociability
Round writing (Palmer method) *(Chapter 14, Figure 139.)*

we generally have guests over frequently

Arcade writing (legibility) *(Chapter 11, Figure 1.)*

I enjoy being with people

Spirituality
Light writing *(Chapter 12, Figure 1.)*

we live our life by the Bible

End strokes ascending upward *(Chapter 9, Figure 23.)*

It is better to give than to receive

Tall upper-zone extensions *(Chapter 14, Figure 70.)*

religion is life

Light, high *i* dots

I work as a volunteer in our local hospital

Stability

i dots and *t* bars evenly (and firmly) written (*Chapter 5, Figure 8.*)
(*Chapter 4, Figure 1.*)

I've worked at my present job for twenty six years

All humps on *m* equal (*Chapter 14, Figure 104.*)

I send some money to my children monthly

Even pressure (*Chapter 12, Figure 3.*)

As a teacher I find it necessary to be calm

Capitals just a bit larger than small letters

I come here every monday with David to get some exercise

Even margin and even base line (*Chapter 8, Figure 6.*)
(*Chapter 7, Figure 1.*)

I find it important that I do certain things every day, I feel that this regulates my life

Vertical (or slightly inclined) writing (*Chapter 2, angle AD.*)

I'll meet you as usual, wednesday at nine, by our favorite restaurant

---

Stupidity

Slow writing

Both my brothers skipped tird glade and I was left back I just can't understand wh

Unharmonious, graceless forms

Why does everybody call me a Dummy?

Submissiveness
Small capitals

Though I should try harder I yield to easily to outside pressure

Small *m*   (Chapter 14, Figure 95.)

I'm just not able to dominate my wife

t bars short and low on stem   (Chapter 4, Figure 27.)

I given whatever they ask of me I'll comply to

Light *t* bars

I find it difficult to be aggressive

Very round writing

If they ask me to leave, I have no choice but to, right?

Light writing   (Chapter 12, Figure 1.)

I am a conscientious objector

i dots very light   (Chapter 5, Figure 12.)

when he asked me to lend him the money, I just felt obligated to

---

Subordination
i dots and *t* bars low placed   (Chapter 4, Figure 27.)

I realize I don't have a chance against him

Small capitals   (Chapter 14, Figure 85.)

since I was a kid I'd always had some kind of inferiority complex

Subordination
Curved, light-pressured writing (Chapter 12, Figure 1.)

I basically look up to everybody

Suicidal tendencies
Lines that cross each other underneath the signature

Louis Carlson

Descending base line (Chapter 7, Figure 3.)

I feel no reason to continue living

Sudden drop at end of line

I find it very difficult to carry . on

End stroke going through capital (Chapter 9, Figure 8.)

Charles

Signature to the left

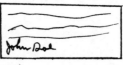

No capitals (especially by name)

I John doe, under no coercion of anyone but the only way out for me is to end it all . signed john doe

---

Superficiality
Concave *t* bars (Chapter 4, Figure 12.)

If we get a chance, will come over and visit you

Garland writing (*Chapter 11, Figure 2.*)

my meetings are mostly meaningless nonsense

Susceptibility

d with looped stem (*Chapter 14, Figure 49.*)

He said he had a million dollars, should I believe him?

Concave *t* bars (*Chapter 4, Figure 12.*)

It's very easy to convince me about anything

Round and light writing (*Chapter 12, Figure 1.*)

wow you really own three yachts & don't even work

Very inclined writing (*Chapter 2, angle AF.*)

whenever he says he loves me I just melt

Tactfulness

Words tapering toward end (*Chapter 11, Figure 5.*)

An idiot always tells the truth, a wise man never lies

Ovals usually closed (*Chapter 14, Figure 114.*)

Somehow or other will work it out

Reclined writing (*Chapter 2, angle AC.*)

I only told them a few words & they busily understood the whole story

Tactlessness

Abrupt terminals   *(Chapter 9, Figure 17.)*

I don't like you, you're stupid, and what's more, you bore me

Words enlarging toward end

my first two husbands divorced me because they said I spoke too much

Postplaced *t* bars   *(Chapter 4, Figure 2.)*

I'm not gonna pay this ticket 'cause you're a stupid cop

Ovals very open   *(Chapter 14, Figure 116.)*

I say everything that's on my mind

Timidity

Very small writing (capitals and small letters about same size).

I don't think I'll be able to do it.

m small (and crowded)   *(Chapter 14, Figure 95.)*

I'm to shy to ask my boss for a raise

Weak *t* bars

I've tried but to no avail to overcome my lack of confidence

Very short *t* bars

To tell you the truth, I'm afraid to go by myself

Light writing   *(Chapter 12, Figure 1.)*

I have all the lights on in my house, all the time

Preplaced *i* dots *(Chapter 5, Figure 7.)*

my lack of aggressiveness has kept me from advancing

Truthfulness
Small letters all basically the same size

Honesty is the best policy

Ovals usually open—but sometimes closed

I find the best way to communicate is to be open and honest

Straight base line *(Chapter 7, Figure 1.)*

I though you've forgotten about it, here's the $100 I owe you

---

Undisciplined behavior
Quick, speedy writing

I love riding on the back of the bus

Poorly spaced

I don't care whose chair that is I'm sitting there

Writing slant often changing *(Chapter 14, Figure 94.)*

I'm eating before you even though you were on line first

Very large writing

I don't like eating with a knife & fork

Crooked base line *(Chapter 7, Figure 5.)*

So hi's you bother, I'll still think he's an idiot

Versatility

Uneven margins   *(Chapter 8, Figure 5.)*

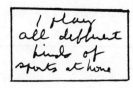

Disconnected writing   *(Chapter 10, Figure 2.)*

Same letters varying in shape

Violence

Club-shaped ascending end strokes   *(Chapter 9, Figure 14.)*

Club-shaped descending end strokes

(Similar meaning of Chapter 8, Figure 38—
end strokes, heavy, descending, pointing.)

t bars thin and then thick   *(Chapter 4, Figure 23;*
                                                                  not necessarily flung down)

t bars long and heavy

You stink, what are you gonna do about it?

Pasty, smeary, muddy-looking (Chapter 12, Figure 4.)

I'm gonna get you when you least expect it

Heavy writing (Chapter 12, Figure 2.)

Pick your things up and get outta here!

Vitality

Long extensions in the lower zone (Chapter 3, Figures 5A and 5B.)

Hey, why don't we climb the mountain without any ropes?

Many exclamation points

really?? wow!!! I can't wait to go to the stadium already!!

Long, heavy *t* bars

I play football every tuesday & thursday

Heavy writing (Chapter 12, Figure 2.)

Handball is my favorite sport

Fast, speedy writing

it's a lot of fun & really healthy to jog

Large writing

I love camping in the woods!

Vivacity
Large writing

I love being alive in your world

p made as a simple stroke   *(Chapter 14, Figure 121.)*

I feel a great / one in the / pypose of living

i dots "dashed" and high

I walk the highwire blindfolded

Long, thin *t* bars

We went iceskating on this real-thin ice

"Crack the whip" *t* bars   *(Chapter 7, Figure 2.)*

I can't tell a joke / though I'm the biggst one of them a

Ascending base line

I'm running up the hill, try and catch me

Vulgarity
Middle hump of *m* highest   *(Chapter 14, Figure 90.)*

My my, do you look atrocious!

Middle hump of *m* pointing downwards   *(Chapter 14, Figure 88.)*

Meet me tonight baby, if you dare!

Ugly-looking capitals   *(Chapter 14, Figure 68.)*

I may be crude, but you're ugly Florence

Muddy, pasty, heavy-pressured writing   (*Chapter 12, Figure 4.*)

I need you desperately honey - right now!

Illegible writing

Come on over to my place sweetie

Poorly spaced

new   york made me   dirty!

Generally "ugly" writing

I'm what you call a dirty old man

Hardly any margin

Here biddie, here's a piece of candy, come on in my car I'll take you for a nice little...

Weak-willed character
Weak *i* dots and *t* bars   (*Chapter 5, Figure 12.*)

I hardly can resist any temptation

Concave *t* bars   (*Chapter 4, Figure 12.*)

It's difficult for me to say no

Will-power
Angular *m*

Regardless of what they may say to me, I've already made up my mind

Abrupt end strokes   (*Chapter 9, Figure 17.*)

I can easily bear the temptation

Willpower

Strong, regular *t* bars   *(Chapter 4, Figure 1.)*

I've made up my mind to start all over again

Strong pressure   *(Chapter 12, Figure 2.)*

I'm determined to win!

Angular writing   *(Chapter 11, Figure 3.)*

Bread isn't good for me, so I simply don't eat it

Worry

i dots resembling dashes   *(Chapter 5, Figure 17.)*

Having not been paid in nine weeks is really getting to me

Descending base line   *(Chapter 7, Figure 3.)*

I'm afraid there may be something wrong with me

Zealousness

Ascending *t* bars   *(Chapter 4, Figure 21.)*

If it's for the cause, I'll do it

Inclined writing   *(Chapter 2, between angles AE and AF.)*

I'd give my life easily for my religion

Left margin widening as it descends

We must
dedicate our
lives for
mankind

Heavy-pressured writing

(Chapter 12, Figure 2.)

Our reward is in the hereafter

16

The Signature

The signature gives graphologists a great deal of information, much more than any other part of a subject's handwriting. The signature *is* the ego, but it goes beyond this point. The body of the writing represents what the writer really is, whereas the signature shows what he would like you to think he is.

If the body of the writing is similar to that of the signature, we see an essentially honest and straightforward individual—one who is not trying to impress others or play a false part. When the signature varies from the body of the writing, graphologists first analyze the body of the writing, to discover what the writer really is. Then they check that against the signature to get an impression of the writer's persona—the role he is trying to play.

FIGURE 1.

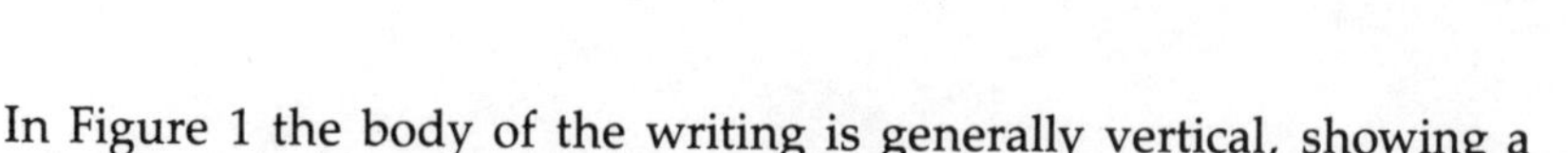

I miss all the grandchildren terribly Grandma Ruthie

In Figure 1 the body of the writing is generally vertical, showing a cool approach toward people in general. The inclined signature implies anything but coolness. Grandma Ruthie wants you to think that she is warmer than she really is.

Notice that the text in the writing of Harriet Beecher Stowe (Figure 1A) is quite similar to that of her signature in angle, pressure, and size of capitals. This consistency between text and signature can also be seen in the writing of Albert Schweitzer (Figure 1B), showing them both to be "true types."

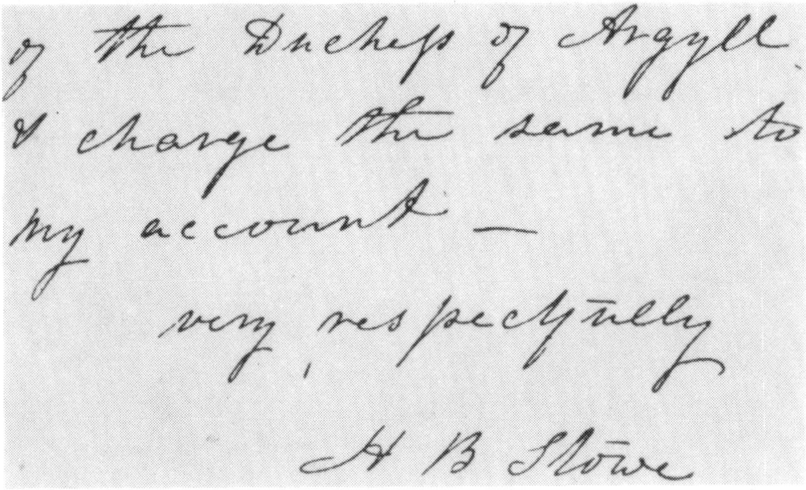

FIGURE 1A.

FIGURE 1B.

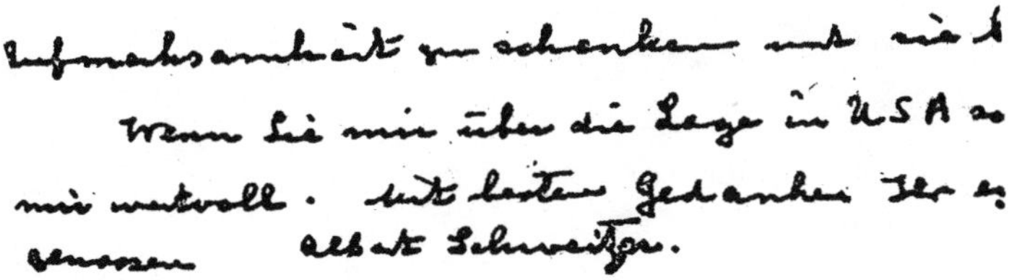

By contrast to Figure 1, Figure 2 shows the body of the writing to be inclined (warm), whereas the signature is more or less upright (cool). Ted is warm and sensitive, but would prefer you to think of him as more indifferent than he really is.

FIGURE 2.

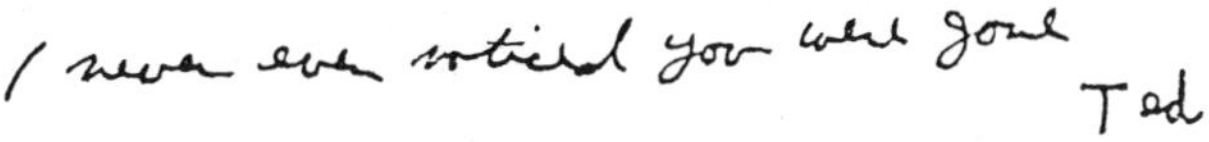

Compare the right-slanted body of the writing of French composer Jules Massenet (Figure 2A) with his vertical signature. The real man was quite warm, but he thought it better for others to think of him as being a bit more "cool," perhaps for professional reasons.

FIGURE 2A.

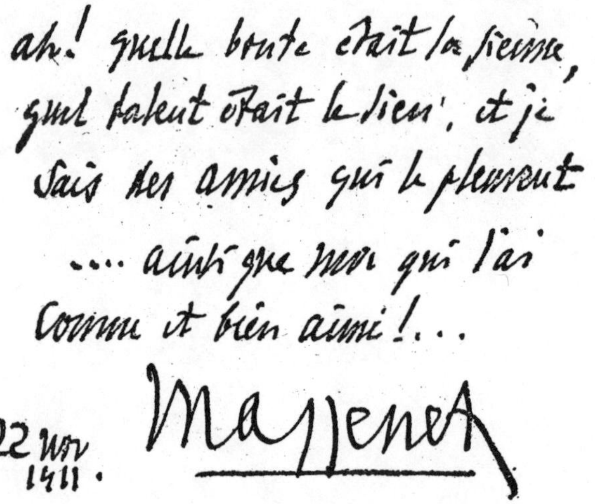

Figure 3 shows simplified writing, but displays an artistic signature. The writer, basically a person of simple tastes, would like you to think she is artistic.

FIGURE 3.

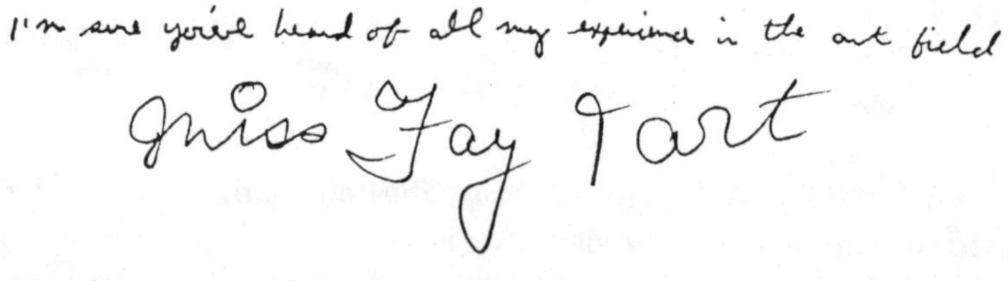

Figure 4 contrasts the large writing of the main body with a tiny signature. The great capital *I* alone shows how highly the writer thinks of himself. Henry Street is far from being humble, but his tiny signature shows that he wants you to think he is.

When a person holds an image in his mind of someone he respects or likes, he tends to make that person's appearance taller than it actually is. The opposite is also true: lack of respect for someone makes him reduce the image in size. These images are shown in his writing.

FIGURE 4.

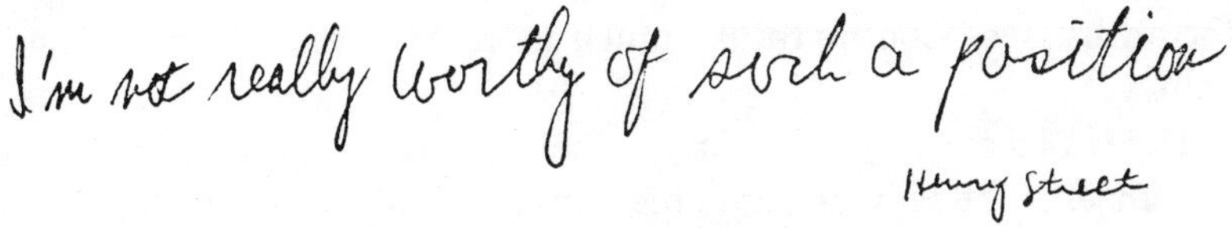

I'm not really worthy of such a position

Henry Street

When the writer in Figure 5 addresses the person to whom she is writing, her handwriting shrinks in size in comparison to the body of the writing. Thus, this writer has low esteem for Mrs. Coll.

FIGURE 5.

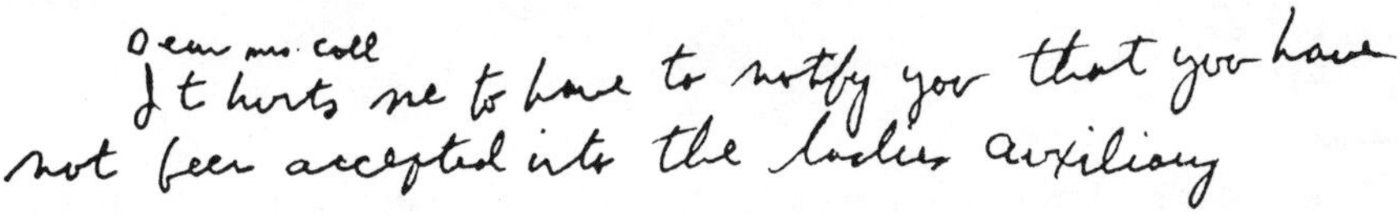

Dear mrs. Coll
It hurts me to have to notify you that you have not been accepted into the ladies auxiliary

FIGURE 6.

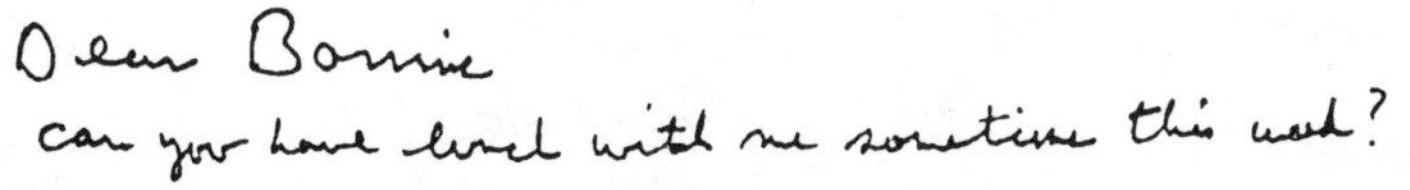

Dear Bonnie
Can you have lunch with me sometime this week?

The body of the writing in Figure 6 is smaller than the name of the addressee. Therefore, the writer has a high regard for Bonnie.

FIGURE 7.

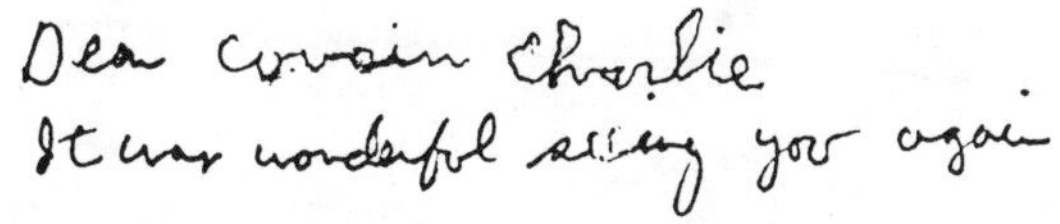

Dear cousin Charlie
It was wonderful seeing you again

Although the addressee's name in Figure 7 is unclear, the body of the writing is quite legible. The writer is confused, not sure of how he feels about his cousin.

FIGURE 8.

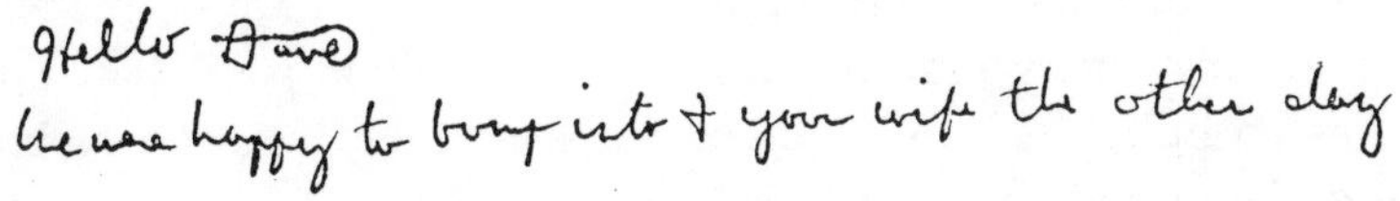

Hello Dave
he was happy to bump into + your wife the other day

In Figure 8, the addressee's name is "wiped out." The writer would love to get rid of Dave somehow or other.

FIGURE 9.

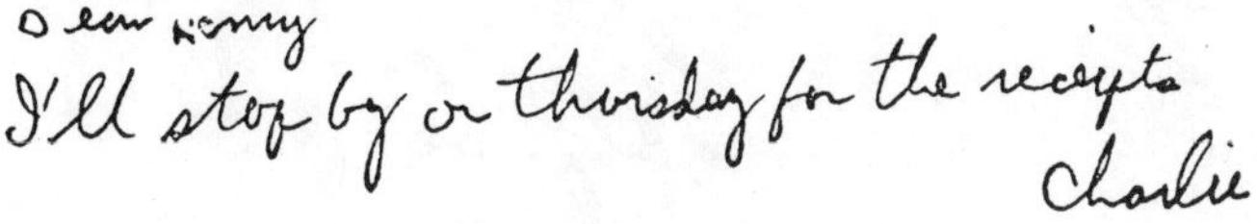

Dear penny
I'll stop by on thursday for the receipts
Charlie

In Figure 9, the writer's own name is written much larger than that of the addressee. Charlie thinks much more of himself than he does of Nancy.

The way a man signs his first name indicates what the writer thinks of himself. The way he signs his surname hints at his feeling toward his family—particularly his father, since the surname does represent him. When both names are equal in size, he demonstrates an equal regard for himself as an individual and for his family. When there is a variation, the writer is portraying how he feels about his relationship with his family.

FIGURE 10.

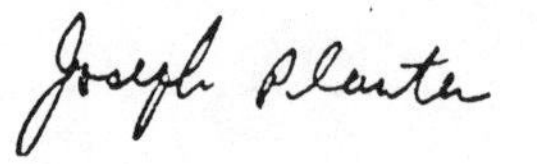

Joseph Planter

In Figure 10, the first name is larger than the surname. The writer is more involved in his own affairs than concerned with being part of his family. This trait can be seen in the signature of Miguel de Cervantes in Figure 10A:

FIGURE 10A.

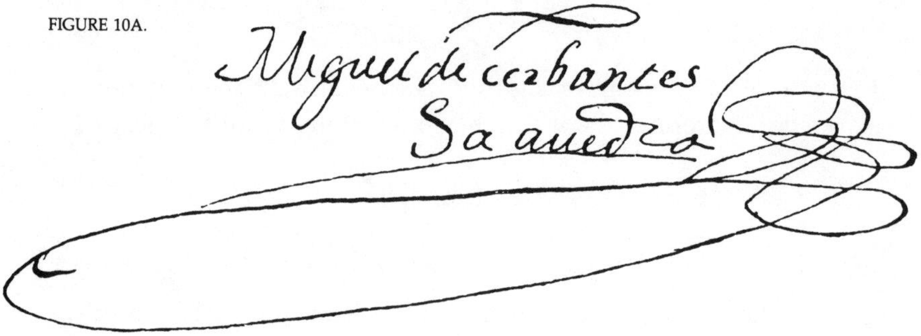

Miguel de cervantes Saavedra

FIGURE 11.

David Lancer

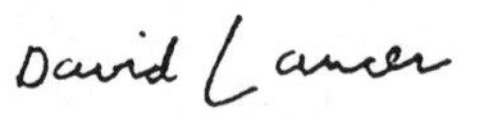

Figure 11 shows the surname larger than the first name. This writer considers his family first and thinks of himself as part of it, rather than as an individual on his own. The signature of Alfred Nobel in Figure 11A shows this trait:

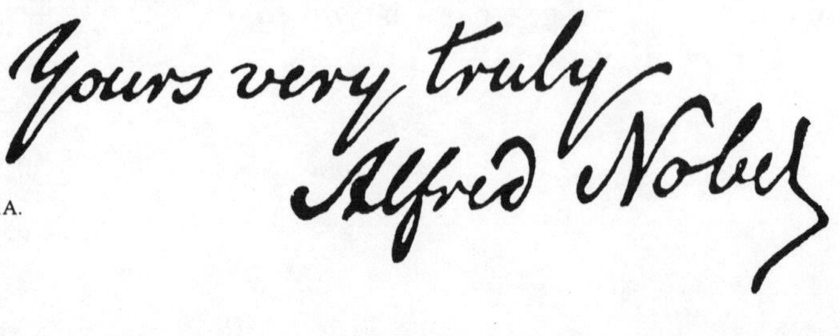

Yours very truly, Alfred Nobel

FIGURE 11A.

When the capitals of both first name and surname are large and relatively even, as in the signature of Ted Kennedy in Figure 11B, it shows a person who is proud of his family as well as himself:

FIGURE 11B.

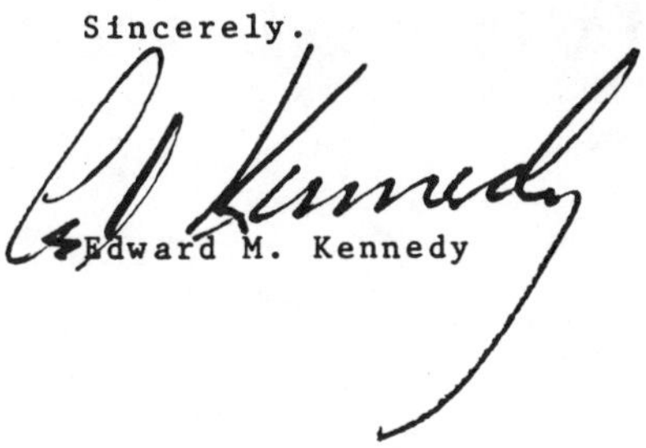

Sincerely.

Edward M. Kennedy

As the following examples show, a woman's writing often demonstrates her opinion toward her husband.

FIGURE 12.

Not only does the woman in Figure 12 sign herself with the title "Mrs.," she writes her husband's name in a large hand. Mrs. Jay is very proud of her Joseph.

FIGURE 13.

In Figure 13 a woman writes her title and husband's last name quite large in comparison to her own given name. She thinks much more highly of her husband than she does of herself.

FIGURE 14.

Though the woman in Figure 14 did sign her name with the title "Mrs.," it and her husband's last name are small in comparison to her own given name. She is prouder of herself than of her husband.

FIGURE 15.

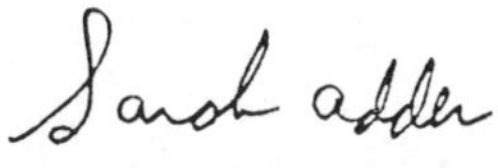

In Figure 15 (this happens to be the signature of a married woman) the writer doesn't show her title of marriage at all, and in addition, she writes her own given name much larger than her husband's. This particular woman is being sued for divorce, and it's easy to see why, since she has so little regard for her husband.

17

Physical Health

Handwriting analysis can often be useful in detecting malfunctions in the body, for there are telltale signs in the ailing person's writing. We know today that although the conscious mind of an individual may not be aware of any particular disorder, on the subconscious level the brain keeps a record of all that takes place in the body. Just as it dictates the personality, so it reacts to the disorder, for it is always aware when something is amiss. If the disorder is repaired, it is interesting to note how the signs disappear from the writing also.

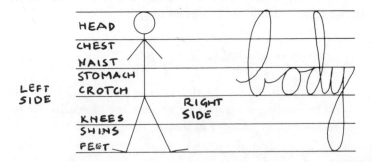

But handwriting signs of physical disorder are not so consistent as those for personality traits. Diagnosing illness through handwriting is still in its infancy. If, for example, a man's left foot is amputated, a gap or blotch may appear in the left side of the lower zone—but only

174

now and then. A normal man would probably not leave gaps there at all, or not with statistically significant frequency. It is this frequency —not a 100-percent consistency—that the graphologist looks for.

FIGURE 1.

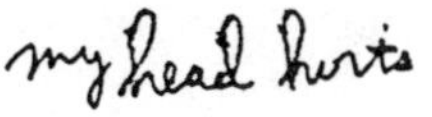

my head hurts

If the handwriting in Figure 1 were superimposed on the stick figure in the above diagram, we would see that the top part of the upper-zone letters would correspond to the head. There are tremulous strokes and even a little gap in one of the letters—all in the same area, the left side of the top of the upper-zone letter. We can easily see why this writer should complain of headaches.

FIGURE 2.

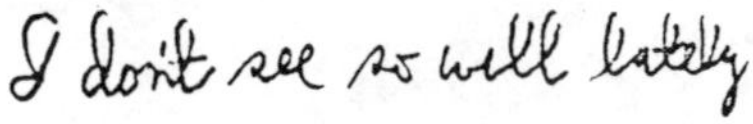

I don't see so well lately

In Figure 2 there are gaps in the right side of the upper portion of the upper-zone letters. This represents the head area, but the gap itself is not located at the top of the letters, but is a bit lower down and here represents the eyes. This writer lost the sight in his right eye.

FIGURE 3

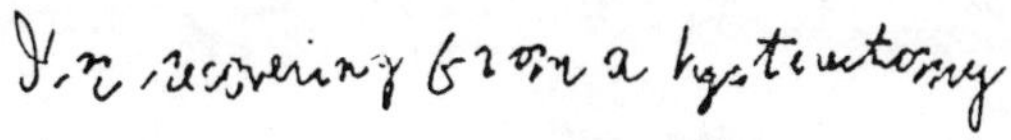

I'm recovering from a hysterectomy

Figure 3 shows gaps in the center of the middle zone, which reflects the area of the stomach and crotch. This woman recently sustained a hysterectomy.

FIGURE 4.

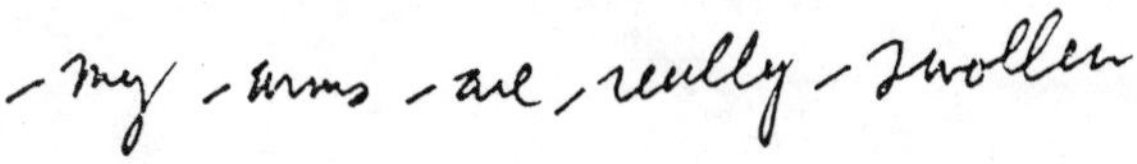

my arms are really swollen

Figure 4 shows middle-zone gaps in the connecting strokes and in the beginning strokes (these gaps can also occur in the end strokes and have a similar interpretation). This area represents the arms and hands. The writer was in an auto accident and his arms went through the windshield; his recovery was not yet complete when he wrote this.

FIGURE 5.

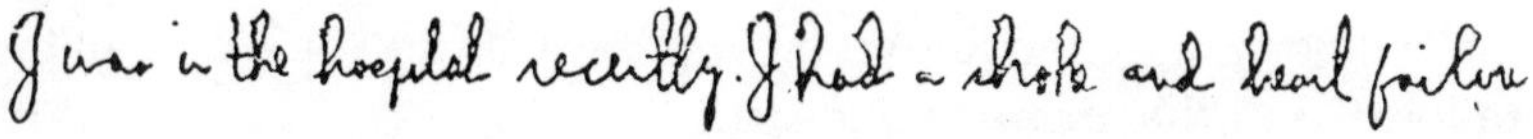

I was in the hospital recently. I had a stroke and heart failure

Most of the defects in Figure 5 appear in the upper left portion of the upper zone. This person had a stroke, which affected the left side of his body. If you look at the *l* in "failure," you will notice that the defect is in the middle part of an upper-zone letter, representing the area of the heart. He also suffered a heart seizure, and the damaged area was found to be on the right side of the heart.

FIGURE 5A.

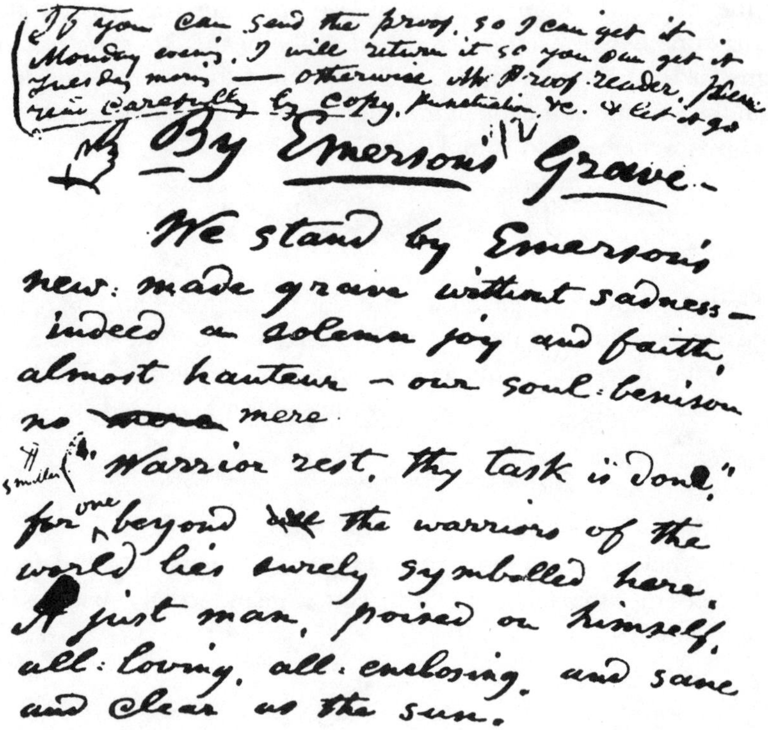
If you can send the proof, so I can get it Monday evening, I will return it so you can get it Tuesday morning — otherwise the proof-reader please read carefully by copy, punctuation &c. & let it go

By Emerson's Grave.

We stand by Emerson's new-made grave without sadness — indeed a solemn joy and faith, almost hauteur — our soul-benison no mere

"Warrior rest, thy task is done,"
for one beyond the warriors of the world lies surely symbolled here. A just man, poised on himself, all-loving, all-enclosing, and sane and clear as the sun.

Figure 5A shows the handwriting of Walt Whitman. Besides having other ailments, Walt Whitman was plagued by a bad heart. To cite only a few examples in this muddy writing (often written by people with poor blood circulation), notice that the *f* in "if" (first word of the first line) has a break in it towards the top, the fourth word of the same line, "send," also has a similar break toward the top of the *d*, the *d* in "Monday" (second line) is broken towards the top—and all these are located in the area of the heart.

FIGURE 6.

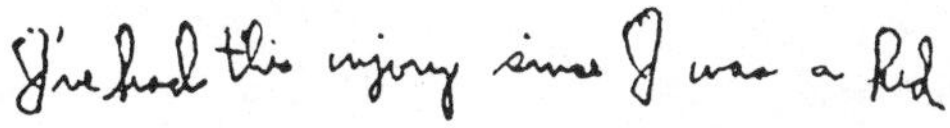

If someone, apparently in the best of health, were to hand you a handwriting sample that looked like Figure 6, you might be a bit reluctant to say that there was something wrong with him. The graphologist should *never* be misled by any outside information whatsoever. Besides certain basic information (age, sex, country of origin), he should get *all* his information from the writing itself. He should not even rely on his own impression; this is not the job of the graphologist. The inexperienced analyst may hear that the subject whom he is analyzing is of a certain type. If he does not uncover this in the writing, he should not make this part of his analysis. Many times, people make untrue statements in order to deceive the graphologist and because they are skeptical. The experienced graphologist prefers that you not tell him anything (except for the above-mentioned basic information), for he does not want his judgment influenced.

The writer in Figure 6 suffered a severe accident when still a child, and part of his left ear was severed. This is indicated by the contrast in his writing. The upper left part of the upper zone is considerably lighter than the rest of the writing. Wherever there is a nick or a space or part of the writing in different pressure from the rest, it is a sign from the brain that something in that particular area is different. This particular defect was not noticeable in the writer's appearance, for his hair was covering it. But his handwriting gave it away.

FIGURE 7.

In Figure 7, we see that there are quite a number of lighter strokes in the middle zone, compared to the rest of the writing. This is often a sign of anemia or low blood pressure—as if the person did not have enough strength to write the word with the proper amount of pressure.

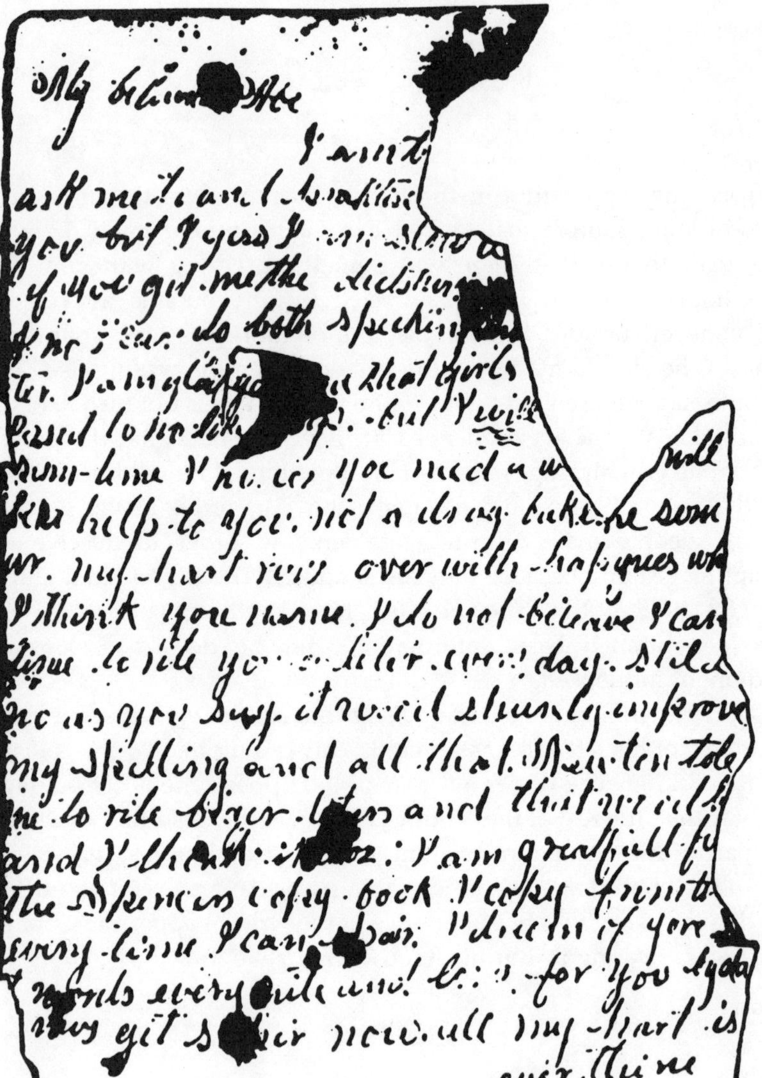

FIGURE 7A.

Lincoln's "true love," Ann Rutledge, suffered from general weakness, as shown here in Figure 7A of her writing—although some of the writing is normal pressure, a considerable amount has almost no pressure at all.

FIGURE 8.

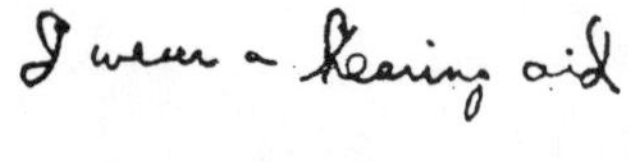

I wear a hearing aid

Figure 8 shows disturbances in the upper right part of the upper zone (reflecting the head)—in two instances a thickening and in one a gap. This person has lost the hearing in his right ear. Why exactly there should be a thickening and a lightening cannot be determined, only that the brain notes a disturbance of some kind.

FIGURE 9.

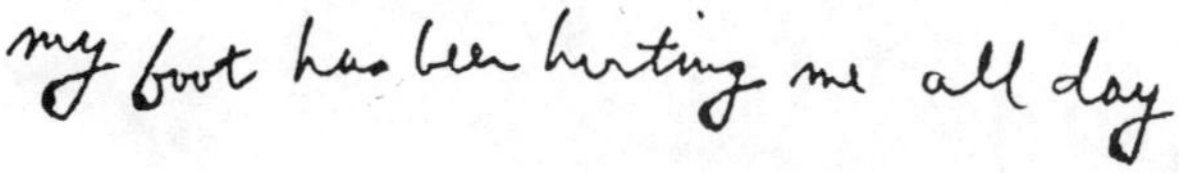

my foot has been hurting me all day

Figure 9 shows heavy pressure in the left lower part of the lower zones (reflecting the feet). This person suffers from corns on her left foot.

FIGURE 10.

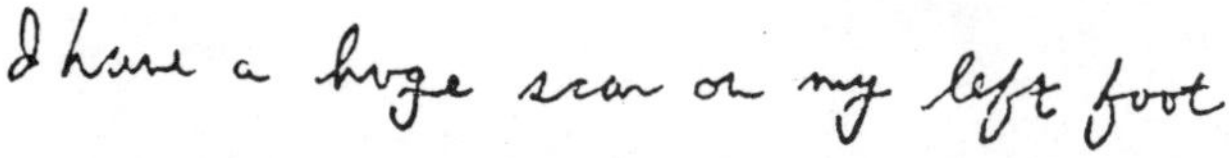

I have a huge scar on my left foot

Figure 10 shows markedly less pressure (almost blank spaces) in the left side of the lower zone. This person was in a fire and still has the scar.

FIGURE 11.

Both my feet are deformed

We see that in Figure 11 both the left side and the right side of the lower zone show empty spaces, areas which correspond with the feet. This writer's feet are both paralyzed—or, as he says, "deformed."

FIGURE 12.

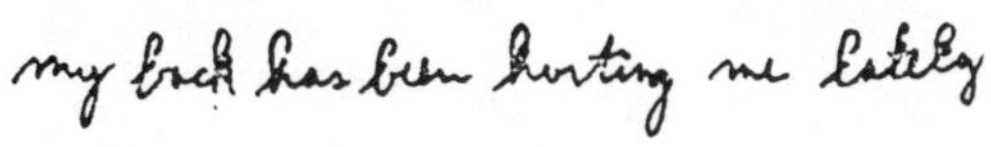

my back has been hurting me lately

The writing disturbance in Figure 12 occurs in the lower part of the upper-zone area (representing the chest-waist area and the back). This writer suffered a slipped disk.

If a person who usually writes in a relatively clear manner suddenly begins to write a blotchy, unclear hand, it is a danger signal of possible physical and/or mental illness. Compare these two handwriting samples of German philosopher Friedrich Nietzsche:

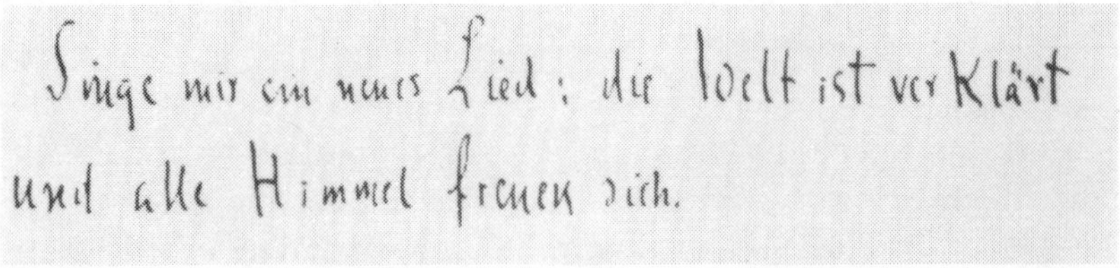

Singe mir ein neues Lied; die Weldt ist verklärt
und alle Himmel freuen sich.

FIGURE 13A.

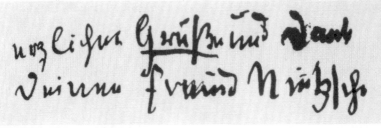

FIGURE 13B.

Though Nietzsche's writing is basically clear in the first sample (Figure 13A), notice the pastose, unclear, blotchy writing of the second sample (Figure 13B), written after his physical and mental collapse.

18

Therapy

There are ways in which handwriting can actually help change the personality. Undesirable traits can be eliminated or changed more or less at will. By writing in a new way, a subject can instruct his brain to produce a new personality.

First the writer must know the graphological signs that indicate the traits in question. If there is a certain trait he would like to eradicate, he simply does not write that way anymore. If there is a trait he would like to acquire, he must know the graphological signs of that particular trait—and train himself to write that way. That's how simple it is.

A word of caution: "simple" does not necessarily mean "easy." A personality trait has usually been with an individual for years, perhaps from childhood, and no one can change overnight. But if the writer sincerely wants to alter a particular aspect of his personality (or several aspects, for that matter) and has a lot of patience, determination, time, and spirit, he can succeed. The therapy in most cases takes a few months—longer or shorter in accordance with the serious intentions of the writer.

Some people might be interested only in getting rid of a negative trait, whereas others might prefer to make a more thorough change and switch over to the positive side. Take, for example, someone who is introverted. He probably displays

1. a left-handed slant
2. preplaced *t* bars
3. preplaced *i* dots
4. knotted ovals
5. small writing
6. light pressure.

If he simply wants to rid himself of his introversion alone, he would change his script to

1. upright writing
2. *t* bar properly placed
3. *i* dot properly placed
4. knot-free ovals
5. normal-sized writing
6. normal pressure.

If he wants to go all the way from introversion to extroversion, he should change his script to

1. a right-handed slant
2. postplaced *t* bars
3. postplaced *i* dots
4. open ovals
5. large writing
6. heavy pressure.

But in addition to this physical change, the writer must make himself feel the mental and emotional change that lies behind it. It's not enough just to retrain his hand, for he is not a robot, devoid of feelings. He must also reset his mind.

The introvert, who formerly wrote with a backhand slant, must be wholly aware that, by writing with an inclined slant, he is drawing himself out of his shell. By unknotting his ovals, he is disentangling himself from the inhibitions that prevented him from being free and open. By enlarging his writing, he is enlarging himself.

Like an athlete body-building in preparation for his performance on the field, the writer should feel he is performing physical, mental, and emotional exercises in acquiring a more desirable personality.

How will the writer know if the new personality has taken effect? When he actually writes the new way without having to think about it, then it has become his natural hand, and he knows that the new personality trait is taking dominance.

It would be advisable to attempt to change only one or two traits at first. More than that may be too burdensome. Moreover, the writer must take into account the total picture. Perhaps this "undesirable" personality trait is troublesome in the short run, but serves an important purpose in his overall life-style. Consider, for example, a man who may accurately be described as stubborn. In private life this trait may annoy his friends, while at the same time it is exceedingly useful in his professional life—as a police detective doggedly tracking down a criminal, say, or as a scientific researcher tenaciously searching for the cure for a disease. In such a case, he would be foolish to try to change himself. The writer must, therefore, weigh the problem carefully and make sure that he isn't throwing out the baby with the bathwater.

Note: If the person frustrates easily, this therapy may not be advisable, since it does require strong nerve. To check on the subject's frustration level, refer to Chapter 5, Figure 5B. Of course, an easily frustrated person may wish to change this trait in himself—but he should be aware of the possible difficulties before undertaking this therapy.

FIGURE 1.

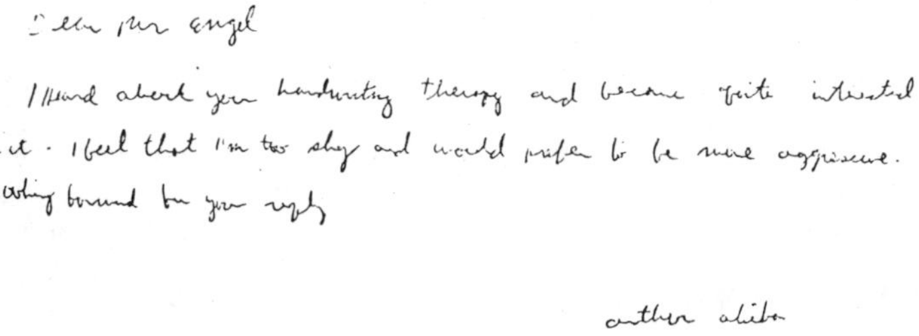

The writer of Figure 1 felt that he was too shy, a trait his handwriting confirmed. He did not want to remain this way, so he sought my assistance in making him a more aggressive individual. The writer was male, twenty-seven years old, and an American. (As we have seen, the analyst must know sex, age, and country of origin in order to carry out an accurate analysis.)

Looking at the handwriting sample, we see very light writing—a major indicator of bashfulness. The capital letters, especially his capital *I*, are quite low—too low for someone who wants to be more aggressive. We also see a frail *t* bar, another indication of shyness. Therefore, we find that the writer's shyness is being corroborated by graphology.

The outstanding factor in this writer's handwriting was his very light pressure. Since the principal writing trait for aggressiveness is heavy pressure, this subject was told to practice writing with heavier pressure, regardless of how difficult it was for him at first. After the writer tried for a few weeks, he sent me a note (Figure 2) letting me know how he was doing.

FIGURE 2.

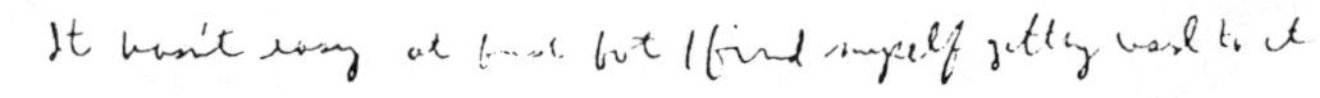

Two months later:

FIGURE 3.

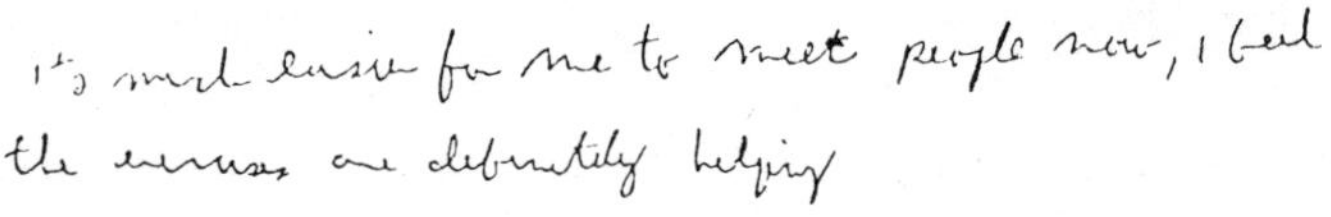

Five months later:

FIGURE 4.

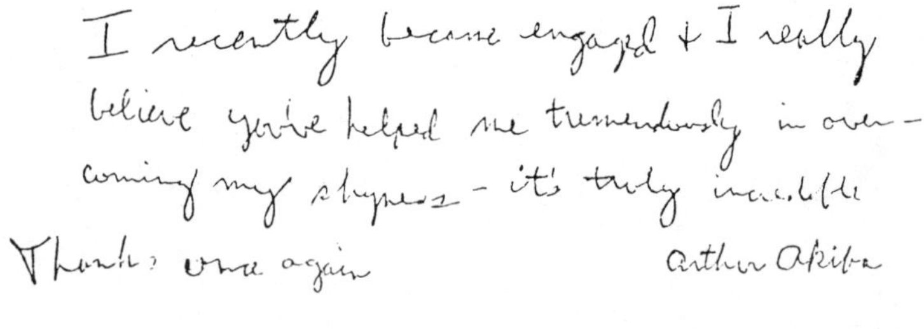

Here, then, are the results. After a few weeks, there was a minimal change—but a change nonetheless—in the pressure. It showed that he was on the right road. Two months later, the pressure was even stronger, but the *t* bars were still too light and the capitals still too low. Five months later, it is hard to believe that this is the same individual who complained about being shy. His writing now is at a good, normal pressure. (We don't want it too heavy, because this would have other implications. We simply wanted a moderate amount of pressure, indicating a moderate amount of aggressiveness).

We also see that the *t* bars are quite firm. The writer himself told us that he noticed it was particularly difficult at first to make his *t* bars heavier. At that point, the writer was still too shy to make strong *t* bars. The capitals are now made at a nice height in comparison to the rest of the writing, and the capital *I* has surely increased in size.

For this writer to be completely cured, however, two more factors would have to be added: angularity and speed. But even at this point, he is doing quite well, and the two missing factors will probably not hold him back by much.

Recently, I received a letter from a young woman who said she was engaged to be married. (He was twenty-nine and an American.) She loved her boyfriend very much, but she felt that he had too little spirituality in him and that this lack might harm the marriage. She forwarded a small note he had written to her and asked us to analyze it and suggest some therapeutic practices that might help him become more idealistic.

FIGURE 5.

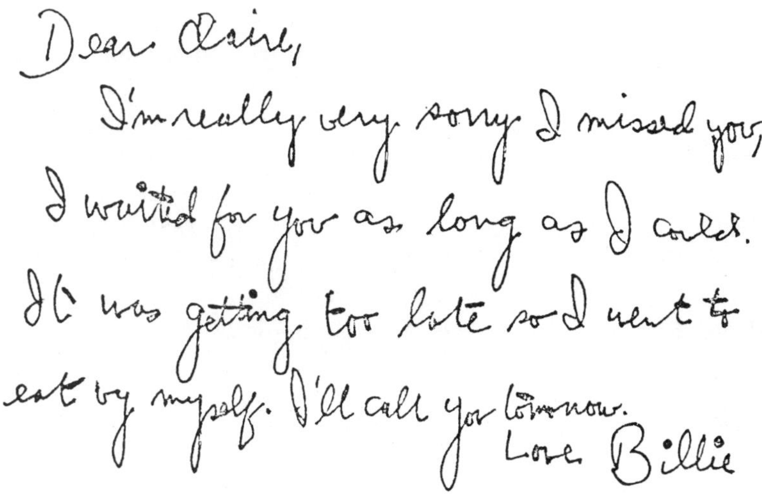

Dear Claire,

I'm really very sorry I missed you, I waited for you as long as I could. It was getting too late so I went to eat by myself. I'll call you tomorrow.

Love, Billie

Looking at Figure 5, we can understand why the young lady was worried, for the handwriting above showed a strong materialistic nature (indicated by several heavy *i* dots, heavy writing, and long loops in the lower zone) and a strong ego (indicated by the large capitals, especially the capital *I*). These negative personality traits prevented spirituality from forming in the writer.

But one major factor outweighed all the others in this particular writing—its heaviness. Heaviness is often quite a positive sign, for it shows drive, determination, strength, and a strong libido. But when the heaviness is combined, as in this case, with pasty, muddy writing, heavy *t* bars that are often flung off the stem and sometimes pointing downward, we see a heavy temper that easily gets out of control.

The young man said he was willing to try to better himself, although he told the girl frankly that he thought writing therapy was a joke. At first, it almost seemed that way, for very little headway was made. But after three months of working at it, this is the way he was writing:

FIGURE 6.

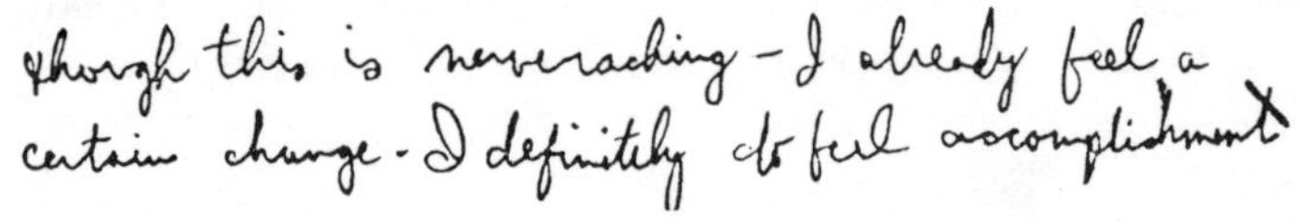
though this is nerveracking - I already feel a
certain change - I definitely do feel accomplishment

Although there is still plenty of work to be done, Figure 6 does show changes. For one thing, the writing is considerably lighter. Light writing is a major component in the handwriting of the spiritual person. Another change is high upper-zone extensions, which seemed to have blossomed in this new writing. (Compare this with Figure 5, in which upper extensions are minimal.) The lower-zone extensions are shorter than they were, giving the writer greater control over himself. One negative aspect still apparent is in the very last letter—the *t* bar is flung down, indicating a certain cruelty.

Three months later, we received this note from the writer:

FIGURE 7.

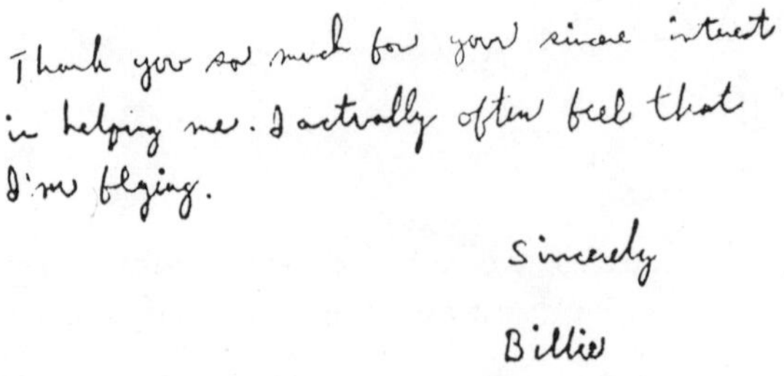
Thank you so much for your sincere interest
in helping me. I actually often feel that
I'm flying.

Sincerely

Billie

Figure 7 is a clear indicator of many improvements. The writing is quite light, and if you compare the heaviness of Figures 6 and 7, the change is quite remarkable. There are no flung-away *t* bars in any direction. They are all centered, showing calmness and control. The upper extensions are now the dominating zone, a major indicator of spirituality. His capital *I*'s are a bit smaller, but healthy, indicating that he has worked on deflating his inflated ego in a healthy manner. A new feature appears: the end strokes ascend, many of them into the upper zone, showing not only spirituality, but mysticism and religiousness as well. Except for the *i* dots, which are still heavy, we see from all the indicators that spirituality is present, a significant change from the man we once knew.

19

How to Do an Analysis

If you should ask any reliable psychoanalyst, "What is a man?" he would probably answer that a man is a composition of everything that ever happened to him. Various occurrences occupy different levels of importance in an individual's life, but, at any given point, every one of them plays a role. When a graphologist is doing an analysis, he must gather every fact and subject it to careful consideration before attributing to it the degree of strength he believes it shares in the personality.

Consider the list of traits (see page 2) that the graphologist analyzes. It would definitely be helpful to the beginning analyst to use this list until it becomes natural to him, so he no longer needs it and can do the analysis without having to refer to it—although the trained graphologist uses this list automatically.

A word of caution: Let the sample writing under analysis tell you the story. Take as evidence only what can be proved from the writing in front of you—it should contain all the facts you require. Whether or not others agree with you, if your analysis is based on the solid facts of the handwriting, then it will be correct.

Don't, under any circumstances, rely on your personal impression of the person who hands you the writing sample. It may not even be his handwriting.

FIGURE 1.

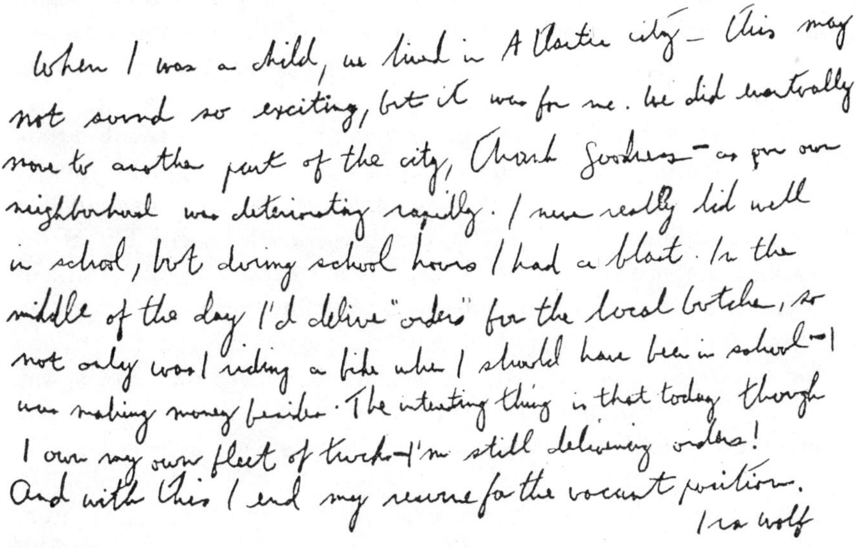

> *When I was a child, we lived in Atlantic city— this may not sound so exciting, but it was for me. We did eventually move to another part of the city, thank goodness—as our own neighborhood was deteriorating rapidly. I never really did well in school, but during school hours I had a blast. In the middle of the day I'd deliver "orders" for the local butcher, so not only was I riding a bike when I should have been in school—I was making money besides. The interesting thing is that today though I own my own fleet of trucks—I'm still delivering orders! And with this I end my resume for the vacant position.*
>
> *Ira Wolf*

Figure 1 was written by a man in his early thirties, who was raised in the United States. Let us go through the list and figure out his personality:

1. *Slant.* There is fluctuation in the direction of the writer's slant. At some points it is almost vertical (AD), at others it moves nearly to the strongly inclined slant (AF), but the majority of the writing is in the lightly inclined area (AE). This high amount of fluctuation in slant shows a moody, changeable nature. When he writes the near vertical hand, he is playing it "cool," but as his slant progresses to the right, a warm, emotional, extroverted, sensitive human being emerges, one who needs people and is reaching out emotionally to others.

2. *Zones.* The upper zone is clearly dominant in this handwriting. The lower zone is also healthy, but the middle zone is small. We see a spiritual, idealistic human being, who is also practical (healthy development of the physical zone represents down-to-earthness, pragmatism). Since his slant is to the right, we see a writer whose aspirations (dominant upper zone) are directed toward the future, a tendency reinforced by the many *t* bars and *i* dots that are placed high and to the right.

When these two facts are combined (high aspirations and rightward slant), we see that the major drive of this individual is inspiration directed toward the future. Many religious people write in this way.

The fact that the middle zone is small reveals a man with strong powers of concentration (further verified by the many exactly placed *t* bars and *i* dots). However, the small middle zone also shows that he lacks confidence, since this zone represents the sociability of the writer. The size of the middle zone is not extremely tiny, but it is dwarfed by the other two zones. This probably means that, although the writer has many sources of strength, it is unlikely that his striving for the future will succeed. His social relationships are not strong enough to sustain him. In order to get where he wants to go, a certain amount of sociability is necessary, and this is what he is lacking.

3. *t bars.* The majority of the *t* bars fall into three types: exactly placed, postplaced, and upward placed. From the exactly placed *t* bars plus the many exactly placed *i* dots, we infer exactness. The exactly placed *t* bars also represent confidence, so although the small middle zone shows some lack of confidence, this lack is not severe. The postplaced *t* bars, plus the postplaced *i* dots, show a quick mind, which can be quite exacting when the occasion demands it. He may like to place his *t* bars and *i* dots exactly, but in situations where he feels exactness is not essential and will hold him back from advancing toward his goal, he will not be too exacting in order to progress.

The upward *t* bars, in addition to corroborating aspirations, show social ambition, since the start of the *t* bar is in the middle zone. This does not contradict the testimony of the writer's small middle zone; it merely hints that, although on one level he shies away from social involvement (probably because he is not exactly sure how to relate to it), he will try to "climb" socially and is afraid of being turned off by others. It is understandable that he should feel inferior in social situations, because when he finally does become involved with a crowd, he spoils it by trying to go over their heads.

4. *i dots.* The *i* dot is the counterpart of the *t* bar, having the same graphological interpretations. When they are found to correspond, we have very strong indications of the particular trait which they represent. Here, postplaced *i* dots match postplaced *t* bars, and the same with exactly placed *i* dots.

However, the *i* dot in this sample has a special meaning of its own. The writer could delete it, and the *i* would still be recognizable as an *i*. (The *t*, on the other hand, would look like an *l* if it were not crossed). The fact that he goes back to dot it exactly shows a keen memory and a strong attention to detail.

5. *Sexuality*. In this writing sample, we have quite a few *g*'s and *y*'s (*y*'s being very close in interpretation to the letter *g*). The upstrokes of these lower-zone letters are approximately equal in length to the upstrokes. Most of the downstrokes measure about 5 millimeters, the upstrokes between 4 and 5 millimeters. We also see that every upstroke goes through the downstroke, which shows completion. So we see 90 percent sexual completion. The majority of the time the writer is basically healthy in this area.

A further verification of this lies in the fact that the downstrokes are not much heavier than the upstrokes. Thus the amount of strength going into the lower (sexual) zone is similar to that spent recovering. A clarification: Most downstrokes, regardless of the zone, are heavier than the upstrokes because the muscles in the hand used to write downstrokes are stronger than those used to write upstrokes. Hence, we only take note of the difference when it is severe.

6. *Base line*. The base line, a major indicator of the mood of the writer, is more or less even here, although it does go above many times and once or twice below. Thus, the general mood of the writer is an average one—that is to say, neither severely elated nor heavily depressed. Quite frequently he has a happy, optimistic outlook on life and at times a slight degree of depression. Therefore, he is not the kind of individual who will get upset easily and is quite reliable and dependable.

7. *Margins*. There are really no margins here, except for a small space on the left. The subject writes all the way to the right edge of the page. Here the accent is on thrift, the wise watching of every penny. The writer rarely, if ever, lets himself go. He may, in fact, be penny-wise but pound-foolish, but is generally consistent in his economies and conservative when dealing with money.

In addition, we note that the writer has no fears of either the past or the future, since he uses up all the space available.

8. *Beginning and end strokes.* Most beginning strokes are missing—the writer gets right into the writing of the letter. Thus, he is direct and requires no springboard. He dislikes people who are devious. He lacks patience, has no time for unnecessary details, and is often short-tempered with others.

The lack of beginning strokes shows a mature writer, who has progressed beyond his school days and the Palmer Method. The letter is perfectly readable without the beginning stroke.

The majority of the end strokes tend toward the right, usually in the middle zone, and are short to average in size. This indicates that the writer gives something of himself to others, although he might give more.

This appears to be a contradiction of our claim (under *Slant*) that the writer has a warm, extroverted personality. But not really. The slant of the writing shows how the subject comes across to people and how outgoing he may be. The end stroke shows how much of himself he is willing to give up. He needs to associate with others, but is unwilling to give much of himself to them. Thus there is an imbalance.

9. *Connected and disconnected writing.* In sum, this writing is firmly connected. Connected writing shows masculine thinking, facts built upon facts (as opposed to feminine thinking, with its many disconnections, allowing intuition to seep through). Thus, this man is a logical thinker, not the kind to follow hunches. He will not make decisions hastily—he is too busy compiling facts—but once he has made up his mind, it will be quite difficult to change it.

10. *Form of connection.* Here we have a combination of three kinds of connection: rounded, angular, and thready. The rounded writing at the bottom of the letters shows an underlying warmth, but since the tops of the letters are quite angular, we also see a lively spirit, one who is alert and competitive and has a critical mind. This writer has a certain amount of aggression but it is tempered by his underlying warmth, which slows down his fast pace.

There is also a certain amount of thready writing here, so we have a person who tends to slip out of difficulties. He does not want to be committed to one course of action. We cannot say that he is diplomatic, because the thready writing is not the dominant form of connection and there are too many open ovals, showing talkative-ness, openness, and honesty. The true diplomat may be lacking in all these traits. Thus, he is merely, on occasion, evasive.

11. *Pressure.* The pressure of the writing is average. Thus there is no overabundance of drive, but enough strength for the basic needs of the writer.

Some of the letters are a bit pasty and muddy-looking, hinting at lust or sensuousness of some kind. If the base line were to descend heavily (which it doesn't), the combined factors of this kind of writing plus depression would indicate alcoholism. Since this individual is not depressed, we see a lust for food. Note that most of the ink-filled letters are located in the middle zone, reflecting the stomach area. This writer derives sensuous gratification from eating. However, not many of the letters are muddy-looking, so lust for food has not run away with him; it is controllable.

12. *Loops.* Most of the upper loops are high and look more like strokes than loops. This, of course, shows idealism, spirituality, a philosophi-cal thinker. But these are not blown-up loops, which hint at materialism and vanity, attempts to catch attention; here we have strokes all but loopless, which implies highly developed intellect in the area of idealism. This personality is not hindered by materialism and vanity, but allows the strong, pure spirituality to take effect.

13. *Letters.* Many of this writer's letters catch the graphologist's eye. The letters are formed simply. Not only is the capital *I* made without flourishes, it is a simple stick. Thus, we see a person who sticks to essentials. The many ovals open at the top show openness, talkative-ness, broad-mindedness, sincerity, honesty. By contrast, the many closed ovals also indicate that the writer has control over his mouth and can keep a secret. Honesty is indicated by the fact that there are both open and closed ovals—he is not hiding anything, but he can keep someone else's secret.

There are also quite a number of *m*'s with the first hump highest. As we know, the first hump of the *m* represents the ego (the self-image of the writer) so there is a healthy self-opinion here. Sometimes there may also be a touch of conceit, but only a touch, because the first humps are not exceptionally higher, and there are many *m*'s where the first hump is not the highest.

We also see some figure-eight *g*'s. These figures represent people with high intelligence, a sign corroborated by the simplified capital *I*, the unlooped upper-zone extensions, and the small middle-zone letters. This is a highly intelligent individual.

14. *Personality traits.* Every personality, however simple or complex, has a multitude of traits. We are interested only in the major ones. The outstanding personality trait of this writer is his superior intelligence, represented by simplified writing (no flourishes, stick-like capital *I*'s, no unnecessary beginning strokes, simple capitals, no elaborations), graceful writing (figure-eight *g*'s), and quick writing (many *t* bars and *i* dots high and to the right).

We also see a lack of confidence, represented by small middle zones. The fact that some *i*'s are higher than others (or not exceptionally small) shows that the lack of confidence is not severe.

The writer's conceit and his lack of confidence are not contradictory in human terms. This writer, in view of his intelligence, sees himself as superior to others, but relating to the crowd is another matter. The shrinking of the middle zone shows a person who is unnerved by close contact with the very people he looks down on.

This writer also changes his slant frequently, showing a lack of consistency on one hand, versatility on the other. The *A* in "Atlantic" is written as a capital *A*, whereas the *A* in "And" (first word of last line) is simply made like a larger lower-case *a*. The word "really" on the fourth line shows two *l*'s in a row, one as a stroke and the other as a loop. Many *g*'s are written similar to the Palmer *g*, whereas others are figure-eight *g*'s. If you look closely, you will notice a slight change of pressure, indicating inconsistency. If the pressure changed severely to the heavier side, we would see a temper that rises suddenly.

Dashes are used excessively in this writing sample, which presents a problem. Dashes represent a very strong indicator that the writer would prefer to keep his distance from the person to whom he is writing. If we found that dashes do not usually appear excessively in this man's writing, we could deduce that he prefers to keep away from something or someone concerned with this particular sample of correspondence, either the person he is corresponding with or the subject about which he is writing. If, however, the dashes appear regularly in his writing, we know that caution is part of the basic personality of the writer. The dashes are seen as "hands" warding off outsiders.

15. *Signature.* There is a certain degree of shaky writing in the signature, but we see some shaking in the body of the writing as well, indicating tension and nervousness. The fact that the signature is very similar to the body of the writing in size, pressure, and slant, with no additional flourishes or exaggerated beginning and end strokes, shows that the writer does not put on airs about himself. He is not a phony, and he is not interested in making a false impression.

16. *Physical health.* There are no gaps and no heavy- or light-pressured spots in any particular part of any letter, and thus no signs of injured or amputated limbs or of malfunctions in the body. The many tremulous strokes show tenseness and a general nervousness, but these conditions are not severe.

20

General Analyses
of Handwriting
Samples

FIGURE 1.

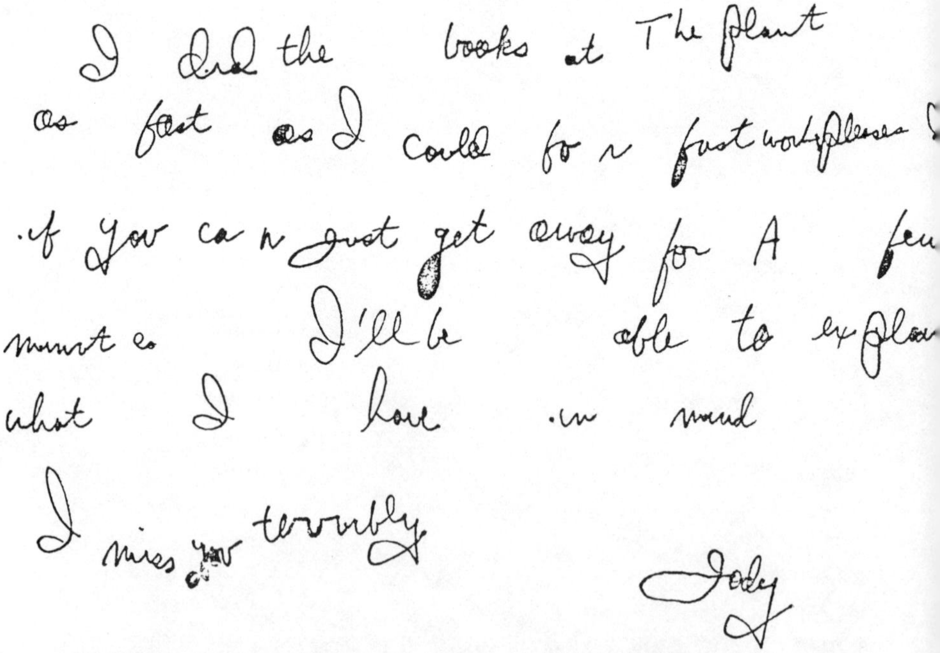

I did the books at The plant as fast as I could for n fast work please if you ca n just get away for A few minut es I'll be able to explai what I have in mind

I miss you terribly

Jody

This handwriting sample was sent to me by a business organization. It shows the writing of a former employee. The personnel manager had always felt this man was somewhat untrustworthy, although he

196

had never stolen anything. Now this man had applied for a job at a branch office of the same firm, and the personal manager felt that, through an analysis of the handwriting, the firm could learn whether it was advisable to rehire him.

The analysis was quite negative.

This is what was uncovered: The writer had an inflated ego, indicated by several very large capital *I*'s and too-wide spacing between the words in comparison to the size of the letters. (The average distance between words should be approximately the size of one middle-zone letter.)

Many of the oval letters are looped and double-looped, and many words contain senseless separations. For example, the word "can" has an irrational disconnection between *a* and *n*. Such separations, whether in words or in spacing between words, show loneliness. The word "minutes" on the fourth line also has this senseless separation, as does the word "for" on the second line.

Senseless separations, whether within or between words, show that the writer is not able to maintain a specific relationship to people. The distances, in the writer's mind, keep others at a safe distance. (Dashes do the same thing.)

There is a lack of rhythm in this sample. The writing itself offends the eye, the up-and-down base line in particular. All these facts—the inflated ego, the too-wide spacing, the looped and double-looped ovals, the senseless separation of words, and the lack of rhythm— add up to one major personality trait: paranoia.

Whenever double loops appear, we know that the writer is probably trying to hide something. So, investigating further, we find pasty, muddy writing, especially in the ovals and the lower zone— the sexual area. We also notice introversion, shown by the many leftward tendencies in the lower zone. The writer has apparently lost control in his "drive." In this particular sample, the letter *p* not only reflects the phallus, it seems to be enclosing it, as though the writer were trying to hide his sexuality.

This writer, a homosexual, was disturbed that his sexual preference might become known. He writes the letter *r* broadly, which shows strong visual qualities. This, along with his paranoid personality, apparently led him to suspect that someone was planning to harm him, and for this reason he left his job suddenly.

Paranoia, of course, is related to fear. But fear itself is represented by cramped, small writing, as though the writer were trying to hide himself in his own skin. Figure 2 is an example of writing showing fear.

FIGURE 2.

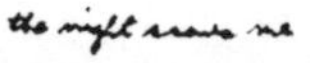

the might scare me

Although fear does not appear in Figure 1, there are other illustrations of paranoia in this handwriting sample. On the end of the second line we see the end stroke extended to the end of the page. This is the kind of person who closes every door with several locks and checks all the switches in the house. There are capital letters where they do not belong—the capital *T* on the first line, the capital *A* on the third line—indicating a certain delusion of grandeur.

Graphology can be very helpful to engaged or married couples, especially when one partner does not understand why the other reacts to a certain situation as he does. Many a wife, noting that her husband seems uninterested in a social life, has inferred that he is ashamed to appear in public with her. An investigation of the husband's writing often reveals that his feelings toward his wife are not involved—he simply does not care much for social life.

A group of young people recently approached me with an interesting challenge. Could it be shown through handwriting which traits were acquired from the father and which from the mother?

The answer is no. If we see signs in a child's handwriting that show him to be a soft, warm individual, and this also shows in the mother's handwriting, we can theorize that he received this personality trait from his mother. If the child's father seems brutal and tough, we can assume that the child does not have his father's personality. But we cannot say just from looking at a person's handwriting whether the traits were acquired from his mother or his father.

21

The Writing on the Envelope

For all intents and purposes, whatever the graphologist needs is in the body of the writing and the signature. The envelope by its very nature, being exterior to the body of the writing, is also exterior to the core of the analysis. Nevertheless, it does shed light on many issues.

The writing on the envelope is quite similar to the signature in that both reflect how the writer wishes to appear. And as with the signature, when we see a variation between the writing in the body of the letter and that on the envelope, we analyze this difference.

A word of caution: A full analysis should never be done from the writing on the envelope alone, but only in conjunction with the body of the letter. In the writer's mind the envelope does not represent his inner self; it is only his relationship to the outside world, his outer self.

FIGURE 1.

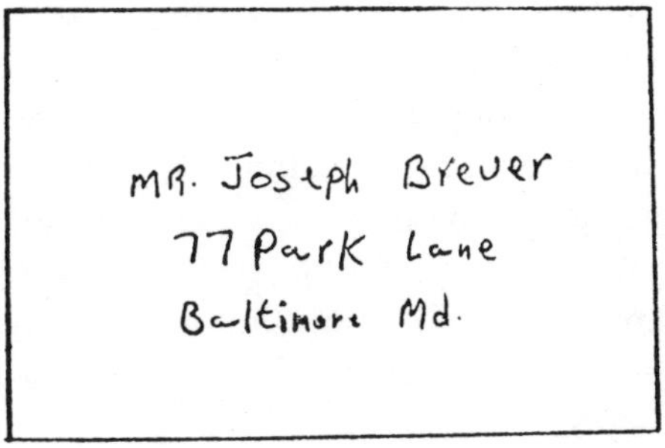

MR. Joseph Breuer
77 Park Lane
Baltimore Md.

One of the major aspects of envelope writing is consideration. The writer wishes his letter to arrive in the hands of the addressee. When we see a neat, legibly addressed envelope, we see consideration for the mailmen and all the other people who have to handle the letter en route to the intended address. Figure 1 shows a letter that is properly addressed and can be read with ease. Figure 2 is much more difficult to decipher:

FIGURE 2.

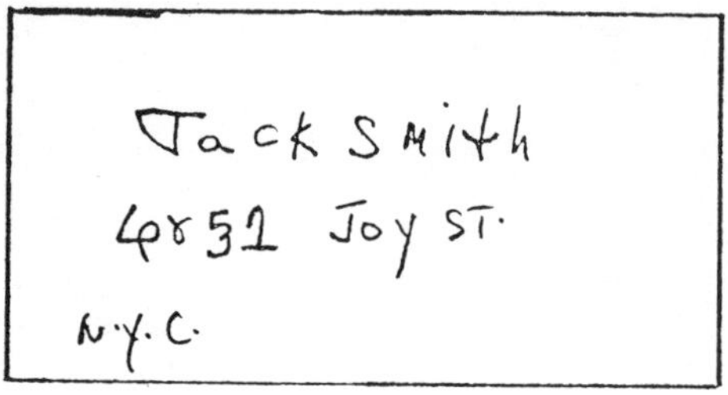

Many people whose writing is normally not very legible make a special effort when addressing the envelope. This is not a significant point for analysis unless the difference is tremendous, for it is only common sense to take pains when addressing a piece of mail. But when we see illegible words and numbers on the envelope, we know immediately that this is a most inconsiderate individual.

Envelope writing usually includes some numbers, which the body of the writing often lacks. Numbers show the writer's relationship to money. People who write illegible numbers are often dishonest. There may be a cheating motivation behind the illegibility—if he is caught, he can say, "I did write the right amount, you just can't read it." The numbers in Figure 2 can easily be misread, and although the writer is not cheating anyone by writing the address so that it is difficult to read, it does reveal that the writing of ambiguous numbers is ingrained in his personality. Whereas the writer of Figure 1 will have an easy time in relating to the outside world, the writer of Figure 2 will always be a quite ambiguous figure to the society in which he lives. He prefers it that way, and the people he meets feel the same way about him. You can have a long conversation with a person like this and afterward realize that you did not understand one word he said.

FIGURE 3.

It would be difficult for an amateur to recognize the body of the writing, which is broad and heavy, from the writing on the envelope in Figure 3. Since the envelope writing reflects the writer's outward behavior, we see that in relating to the outside world, he is shy and lacks confidence, whereas to the people he knows best, he is quite self-assured.

FIGURE 4.

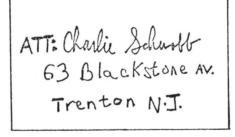

The body of the writing of Figure 4 is quite light in comparison to the heavy writing presented here on the envelope, so this man is the opposite of the writer of Figure 3. Though he wants the outside world to think that he is self-confident, he really is quite unsure of himself.

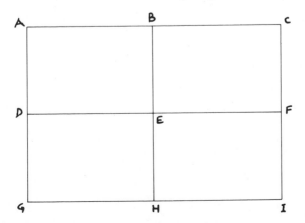

Taking envelope writing alone, without comparing it to the body of the writing, we consider just the placement of the address. When we see a letter that is addressed in the middle—that is, on or near the lines DEF and BEH in the diagram shown here—we see mental balance. There are no serious extremes in the writer.

The area ACFD reflects the upper zone, and area DFIG corresponds to the lower zone. Area BCIH reflects the right (inclined) slant, and area ABHG reflects the left (reclined) slant. Each area can be interpreted in accordance with its corresponding zone or slant.

Area BCFE corresponds to the right area of the upper zone, showing mental activity, but intense emotion as well, a combination that produces a general lack of self-control.

Area ABED corresponds to the left area of the upper zone, so we see a withdrawn person, not only living in the past, but having a fear of the future.

Area EFIH corresponds to the right part of the lower zone, and shows an aggressive, materialistic personality.

Area DEHG corresponds to the left part of the lower zone and shows a cautious, repressed individual, one whose instincts and sexuality are inhibited.

22

The Famous and the Infamous: Five Analyses

For the Government of the
Arab Republic of Egypt:

For the Government
of Israel:

عن حكومـة
جمهورية مصـر العربيـة :

عن حكومـة
اسرائيـــل :

בשם ממשלת הרפובליקה הערבית
של מצרים :

בשם ממשלת ישראל :

Witnessed by:
شَـهد التوقيــع :
הועד על-ידי :

Jimmy Carter, President
of the United States of America

جيمـى كارتــــر ، رئيــــــس
الولايات المتحــــدة الأمريكيــــة

ג'ימי קארטר, נשיא
ארצות הברית של אמריקה

On March 26, 1979, the Israeli-Egyptian Peace Treaty was signed in Washington. The signatories representing their respective governments were the Prime Minister of Israel, Menachem Begin, and the President of Egypt, Anwar Sadat. President James Earl Carter of the United States witnessed the signings. Let us observe the Israeli Prime Minister's signature. The smallness indicates a modest demeanor. The exactly placed *i* dot shows precision, a factual personality. Notice Mr. Begin's return stroke of the *g*; instead of the normal path, to the left and up, it goes the opposite route, to the right and up; this shows altruism. I have seen several of the Prime Minister's signatures and have always noted this same phenomenon. The strongly descending second stroke of the *n* shows that he feels himself to be on the defensive, dipping into the lower zone for additional strength to hold on to his views.

Now let us examine the Egyptian President's writing. The signature is unclear, so I have included a thank-you note (Figure 2) Mr. Sadat wrote to the King David Hotel after his visit to Jerusalem.

FIGURE 2.

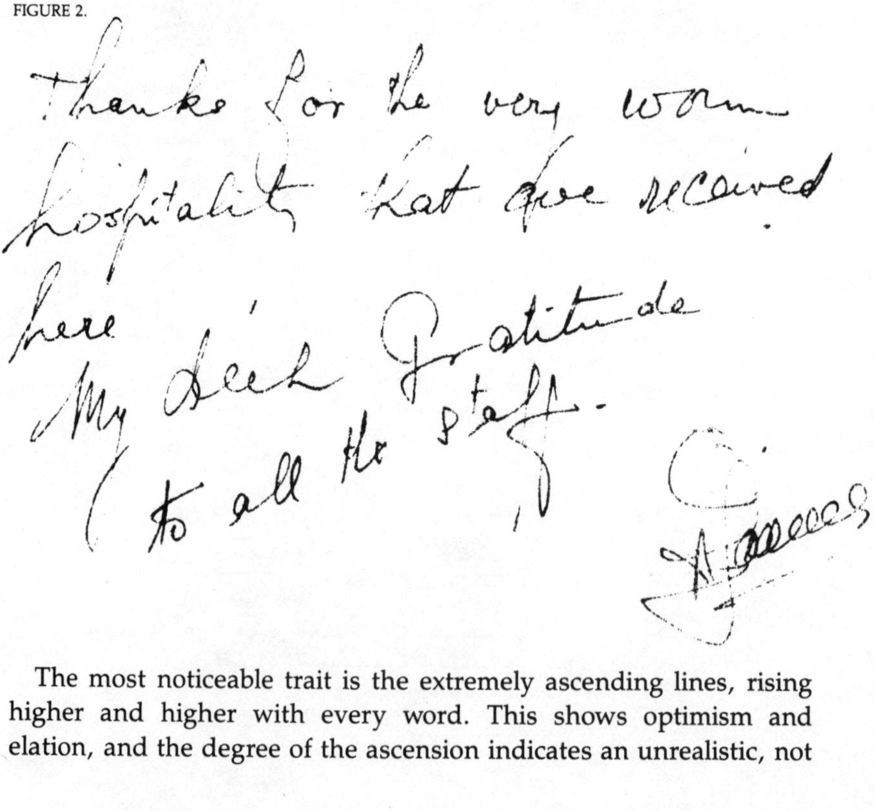
Thanks for the very warm
hospitality that we received
here
My deep Gratitude
to all the staff.

The most noticeable trait is the extremely ascending lines, rising higher and higher with every word. This shows optimism and elation, and the degree of the ascension indicates an unrealistic, not down-to-earth personality. It is easy to see why his people should believe in him so strongly, since these rising lines emit a feeling of exaltation. People naturally want to follow such an enthusiastic leader.

His *t* bars hint at obstinacy—in particular, the first letter in "thanks." Not only does it begin with a hook, it also ends with one; if he wasn't stubborn enough at the start, he was at the finish. In the word "warm," the last word of the first line, the end stroke extends outward, showing generosity, an extension of himself. Then suddenly something happens; he cuts this off sharply, as if saying, "Hold it, I've changed my mind." A prediction?

What was President Carter's real role, standing between the two leaders? What was going through his mind? Let's examine his writing:

The slant to the right shows warmth, a leaning toward people. His diplomacy is revealed in the diminishing size of his middle-zone letters. In Mr. Carter's surname, the last two letters, *er*, are clearly smaller than the first two middle-zone letters, *ar*—a sure indication of the diplomat. Strong intuition is indicated by the many breaks in his name. Concentration and fatalism are indicated in the downstroke of the *y*, which has no return stroke. With his enormous capital letters J.C., does he feel that, by playing "peacemaker," he is the protagonist in a messianic dream?

Here are two sample writings of Adolf Hitler:

FIGURE 3A.

FIGURE 3B.

It has many peculiar aspects.

1. *The slant.* By measuring Figure 3A with a protractor you will notice that the capital *M* measures 28 degrees of incline; at the end of his name, the incline has become an acute 14 degrees. (Any slant measuring under 55 degrees must be considered pathological.) Not

only does Hitler's writing start out pathologically, it becomes more so as it continues. His last letter is almost horizontal. Remembering that slant indicates the degree of approach to others, we see here an intense need of some kind—a desperate grab toward his fellowman. The fact that the writing looks as if it were falling shows acute depression.

2. *Pressure.* The extreme pressure in both specimens indicates a powerful, physical dynamo of energy when dealing with his fellowman.

3. *t bars.* In Figure 3B, we see a thick, heavy, brutal-looking *t* bar, written in a downward direction. This *t* bar shows us how *Der Führer* approaches the addressee. Hitler's down-flung *t* bar, written with heavy pressure (even without his acutely inclined writing) leaves us in no doubt how he could become the monster that he was. We should also remember that the down-flung *t* bar indicates the writer's low opinion of others. It wasn't difficult for Hitler to do away with people.

4. *Capital letters.* The name *is* the ego, and any capital letter also indicates the writer's ego state. Consequently, the capital letter of the name has an especially important meaning in interpreting the writer's ego.

Look at both 3A and 3B. The name is already written with a thick hand. Then Hitler adds something quite unnecessary to the capital in his surname—a vertical bar. This ugly, vulgar-looking, heavy,

FIGURE 4.

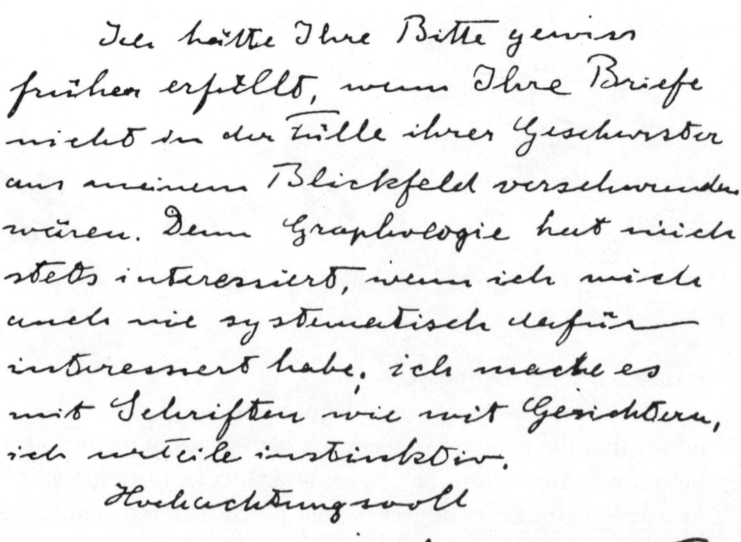

Ich hätte Ihre Bitte gewiss früher erfüllt, wenn Ihre Briefe nicht in der Fülle ihrer Geschwister aus meinem Blickfeld verschwunden wären. Denn Graphologie hat mich stets interessiert, wenn ich mich auch nie systematisch dafür interessiert habe. ich mache es mit Schriften wie mit Gesichtern, ich urteile instinktiv.

Hochachtungsvoll

Albert Einstein.

down-flung line, a tasteless ornamentation to an already ugly character, proclaims a deformed and depraved ego. If the world had recognized this depravity in his writing before his rise to power, would it have made any difference? One wonders.

How does the writing of Albert Einstein reflect genius? It looks so simple! The truth is that simplicity is one of the keys to superior intellect.

A small middle zone is necessary for high powers of concentration. At some points, Einstein's middle zone becomes microscopic. Notice how extremely even the left margin is as it descends, showing a sense of order. Add to this the many exactly placed *i* dots, and we have an extreme sense of order and an exacting memory. Cautious by nature (also indicated by the exactly placed *i* dots), Professor Einstein adds a dot after his surname—just as a precaution. His clearmindedness and creative ability are shown by not allowing one letter to protrude into another in the lines above or below.

Yet the most striking characteristic seems to be his *t* crossings. Observe their individualistic, even strange, maneuverability in the upper (intellectual) zone. It is as difficult to describe what Einstein does in this region as it is to define genius.

Bibliography

Colombe, Paul D. *Grapho-Therapeutics: Pen and Pencil Therapy.* New York: Popular Library, 1966.

Lucas, DeWitt B. *Handwriting and Character Analysis.* Bridgeport, Conn.: Associated Booksellers, 1959.

Mendel, Alfred O. *Personality in Handwriting: A Handbook of American Graphology.* New York: Ungar, Frederick, Publishing Co., Inc., 2nd ed., n.d.

Olyanova, Nadya. *Psychology of Handwriting.* North Hollywood, Cal.: Wilshire Book Co., n.d.

Paterson, Jane. *Interpreting Handwriting.* New York: McKay, David, Co., Inc., 1977.

Roman, Klara G. *Handwriting: A Key to Personality.* New York: Pantheon Books, 1977.

Singer, Eric. *Manual of Graphology.* New York: Hippocrene Books, 1975.

Wolff, Werner. *Diagrams of the Unconscious: Handwriting and Personality in Measurement, Experiment and Analysis.* New York: Grune & Stratton, Inc., 1948.

Index

211